DAIRY FOOD
for all seasons

COMPILED BY
JENNENE PLUMMER

NUTRITION CONSULTANT
PAULINE HOLDEN

BayBooks
An imprint of HarperCollins*Publishers*

A BAY BOOKS PUBLICATION
An imprint of HarperCollinsPublishers

First published in 1993 in Australia by Bay Books, of
CollinsAngus&Robertson Publishers Pty Limited (ACN 009 913 517)
A division of HarperCollinsPublishers (Australia) Pty Limited
25 Ryde Road, Pymble NSW 2073, Australia

HarperCollinsPublishers (New Zealand) Limited
31 View Road, Glenfield, Auckland 10, New Zealand

HarperCollinsPublishers Limited
77-85 Fulham Palace Road, London W6 8JB, United Kingdom

National Library of Australia
Cataloguing-in-Publication data:

Dairy food for all seasons
Includes index
ISBN 1 86378 036 X.

1. Cookery (Dairy Products). I. Plummer, Jennene.
(Series: Bay Books cookery collection)
641.67

Chapter opener and front cover photography by Quentin Bacon
with styling by Jennene Plummer
Food Editor: Jennene Plummer
Nutrition Consultant: Pauline Holden

ACKNOWLEDGEMENTS

The publisher would like to thank the following people and organisations for their
assistance during the production of this book:

The Australian Dairy Corporation for supplying recipes, photographs and
nutritional information.

Yvonne Webb for the following recipes (© Yvonne Webb):
Rich Honey Ice cream, Coffee Ice cream, Iced Strawberry Soufflé, Yoghurt Honey
Ice, Chocolate Sauce, Butterscotch Sauce, Warm Fudge Sauce, Cold Coffee Sauce,
Apple Yoghurt Ice, Basic Vanilla Ice Cream, Chocolate Gelato, Strawberry Gelato,
Banana Ice Cream, Continental Chocolate Ice Cream

Lesley Howard Murdoch and Mark Young for the following recipes (© Lesley
Howard Murdoch and Mark Young):
Stuffed Eggs, Cottage Cheese Patties, Crumbed Chicken in Butter, Chocolate Torte,
Sweet Twists, Flaky Pastry, Strudel with Pears and Apples, Yeast Buns, Flat Bread,
Sour Cream Biscuits

Printed by Griffin Press, Adelaide
Printed in Australia
5 4 3 2 1
97 96 95 94 93

Contents

Introduction 4

Dairy Food with Fruit 10

Dairy Food with Vegetables 22

Dairy Food with Eggs 34

Dairy Food with Pasta & Rice 44

Dairy Food with Meats & Seafood 54

Sweet Dairy Tastes 66

A Baker's Dozen 82

MEASURING MADE EASY 94

INDEX 96

DAIRY FOOD FOR ALL SEASONS

Dairy foods include milk, cheese, butter, cream and yoghurt. They are an important part of the daily diet, both culinarily and nutritionally.

They provide dietary calcium, protein, riboflavin and vitamin A in a digestible, natural form. People trying to lower their fat intake can still enjoy these delicious foods by using low fat alternatives, now readily available.

In the kitchen, dairy foods are invaluable for their unique flavours and textures plus the integral part they play in many cooking procedures.

• Milk, available in full cream, skim, UHT, reduced fat, low fat, flavoured, cultured (buttermilk), canned and powdered varieties, is nature's most important drink and features extensively in cooking.

• Cream, whether pure, thickened, sour or reduced, adds a touch of luxury to many dishes. Light versions are now also available.

• Butter, made from churned, fresh, pasteurised cream, is available unsalted, cultured and in blends for ease of spreading.

• Yoghurt, a cultured milk product, is available plain, low fat or flavoured.

• Cheese is one of the most natural, versatile and convenient dairy foods. It is a concentrated source of nutrients, especially calcium. Hundreds of varieties provide a tantalising choice.

• Ice cream, an all time favourite, available in full cream or low fat varieties and in many flavours.

The recipes featured in this book offer a superb collection of ideas blending these delicious, versatile foods with fruit, vegetables, eggs, seafood and meat, pasta and rice.

Many wonderful sweet creations and mouthwatering baked goodies are also featured to tempt just about everyone.

Dairy Food for all Seasons is a complete guide to cooking with dairy food for all occasions. Our hints and tips and nutritional information will be of great help and interest to everyone who enjoys food and cooking. Recipes which are especially low in fat and cholesterol or with low fat alternatives suggested are marked with this symbol: ⚖

MILK

Milk is fresh, contains no additives and comes in different forms to suit different tastes and lifestyles. It provides essential nutrients — carbohydrate for energy, body building protein, calcium and phosphorus for bones and teeth and many vitamins. For this reason it is invaluable in the diet for the growing child, expectant and breastfeeding mothers, senior citizens, teenagers and adults.

There are now a wide range of milks available. These milks can be used as they are or in drinks, soups, sweet and savoury custards, batters, sauces, casseroles, ice creams, drinks or whipped gelatine desserts. Remember though, that low fat milks do not have the same thickening or setting properties as full cream milk. Sauces are thinner and custards produce weak gels.

Milk may be full cream, longlife, skim, modified (either reduced fat or low fat), flavoured, cultured, canned (evaporated — full cream or reduced fat; condensed — full cream or skim) or powdered (full cream, low fat, skim).

Full cream milks must have a minimum of 3.2% milkfat; reduced fat milks between 1% and 2% milkfat, low fat milks not more than 1% fat and skim milk, not more than 0.15% milkfat. Longlife (or UHT — ultra heat treatment) is heated to 132°C (260°F) for 1 to 2 seconds and then sealed in special packaging. This milk will keep without refrigeration for up to 5 months if the packaging remains sealed, except under adverse storage conditions. Once open, it must be refrigerated and the shelf life becomes equivalent to fresh milk.

Modified milks are a mixture of milk, skim milk, milk powders and various combinations of milk products. These milks may be low fat, high calcium, high protein, low lactose or other combinations.

Evaporated milk is milk evaporated to increase solid content to at least 28%. This milk also often has sugar added, making sweetened condensed milk.

Buttermilk is traditionally a liquid by-product of butter making. Today it is a cultured and manufactured product made by adding certain bacterial cultures to pasteurised skim milk.

The amount of milk we need depends on age, growth and activity level. On average, children require about 600 ml per day; adolescents require about 600 to 900 ml per day; adults about 450 ml per day; pregnant, breastfeeding, postmenopausal women 900 to 1000 ml per day.

LACTOSE INTOLERANCE is the inability to digest the natural sugar (lactose) in milk and milk products. It is not an allergy. Symptoms include bloatedness, flatulence and stomach pain. Up to 70% of the world's population is naturally lactose intolerant, possibly as a result of their cultural background (Asian), which has not involved a reliance on milk for nutrition after childhood. Also, some people become intolerant for a week or so after a gastrointestinal upset. Symptoms improve and gradually milk can be tolerated again.

Those people who are lactose intolerant can still consume some dairy food. There are some low lactose milks and all cheese (except ricotta) contains small amounts of lactose. Also, yoghurt is usually fine, due to the bacteria digesting the lactose. Lactose reducing drops and tablets are also available.

Tolerance can increase by drinking a little milk with meals or drinking small amounts of milk throughout the day.

MILK IS PASTEURISED (heat treated to kill any bacteria) and **HOMOGENISED** (the fat is finely distributed through the milk).

Regular milk is great for toddlers and families. Reduced fat and low fat milks are good for adults and older children on low fat or low cholesterol diets. Those milks enriched with extra calcium are perfect for people with high calcium needs.

A very small number of people develop allergy to milk. Most children grow out of this by the age of 4 as their bodies and immunity mature. It is rare for adults to be allergic. Milk allergy should not be self diagnosed. It needs management by a doctor or dietician.

YOGHURT

Yoghurt is one of the most complete foods available and is a palatable, nutritious and easily-digested food, which is used in a great number of recipes in its plain form. Commercially, yoghurt is made by adding bacteria to milk. This converts the sugar in milk (lactose) to lactic acid which sets it into a soft curd, by coagulating the protein in milk.

You can purchase yoghurt in natural (plain) or flavoured varieties, where sweeteners, flavours and fruit pieces are stirred through the natural yoghurt during manufacture.

Natural yoghurt contains 3.4% fat, reduced fat yoghurt contains 1.7% fat and low fat yoghurt contains 0.2% fat.

Add tang to many dishes by adding natural yoghurt in some of the following ways:
• Use it to finish off a curry.
• Blend it with herbs, spices, garlic or cucumber to make simple sauces, dips or dressings.
• Use it in place of sour cream.
• Use it in place of milk in some cake, scone and cookie recipes.
• Blend it with honey, nuts or fruit pieces to make your own flavoured yoghurt and a great, quick and simple dessert.
• Spoon it on cereal as a change.
• Eat it on its own or with fruit.

Yoghurt is simple to make, wholesome, delicious and a good source of protein, vitamins and minerals. Its fat level depends on whether you make it with whole, skim or reduced fat milk.

Cultures for making your own yoghurt may be purchased in dehydrated form in packets from health-food shops or simply use a spoonful of yoghurt to introduce the bacteria to warm milk. Choose a plain yoghurt, relatively free from additives (read the label carefully). Each time you make a batch, save a spoonful to start the next one. If, after several batches, the yoghurt does not taste as good or set as well, begin the process again with a new batch of culture or a new tub of bought yoghurt.

MAKING YOGHURT

EQUIPMENT You need either a yoghurt maker or a thermos flask for making yoghurt. There are two basic types of yoghurt makers on the market. Electric ones have an element which will heat the milk to the right temperature and keep it there while the yoghurt sets. They come either with a large pot to make one large batch or with small pots for individual servings. The single batch type tends to have the advantage, especially if you want to thicken your yoghurt. Insulated yoghurt makers simply keep warm milk at a constant temperature until the culture matures.

If you do not want to buy a yoghurt maker, use a thermos flask, preferably one with a wide mouth, or a clean glass jar. Just stand it in a warm place where the temperature is fairly sure to stay around 35°C (65°F) to 45°C (85°F). You will also need a cooking thermometer if you are not using an electric yoghurt maker.

METHOD

Making yoghurt is very simple. Just follow these directions, leaving out steps 1 and 2 if you have an electric yoghurt maker.

1 Heat 1 litre of milk in a saucepan or your microwave to 85°C (170°). (Be careful if using your microwave. It will take about 10 to 12 minutes on high to heat 1 litre of milk. Watch it carefully in the final stages to see that it doesn't boil over.)

2 Allow it to cool to 43°C (80°F) to 45°C (85°F).

3 Stir in 1 tablespoon of fresh, plain yoghurt.

4 Put the mixture into a yoghurt maker, flask or jar and set aside for between 5 and 12 hours, depending on how sharp you like the flavour. The longer you leave it, the sharper it will be.

5 When it has set and matured to your taste, store it in the refrigerator.

HOW TO MAKE THICKER YOGHURT

Many recipes use yoghurt just as it sets. However, for some recipes or for eating, it is nicer if it is thicker. If you are using dried skim milk to make your yoghurt, experiment by increasing the milk powder until you get the consistency you like. (Try filling about one-third to a half of your container with powder and top it up with water.) If you are using fresh milk (full cream or a low fat variety) you can thicken the yoghurt by adding milk powder as well. However, the best way to thicken yoghurt is to drain it for about 4 hours after it has finished setting. This yields a smooth, creamy-textured yoghurt.

To drain yoghurt you need a bowl (stainless steel or glass) and a colander which fits over it. Line the colander with a clean piece of cheesecloth or cotton sheeting (sterilised) then pour the fresh yoghurt into it. Leave in the refrigerator for about 4 hours or overnight, if you like it really thick. If you forget to take it out and it becomes too thick for your liking, don't worry. Stir back some whey, 1 tablespoon at a time, until you have the consistency you want.

CREAM

Cream (pure or whipping cream) ranges in milkfat content from 35% to 48%. Reduced creams have a minimum of 25% and light creams have a minimum of 18% milkfat.

Cream is available pure, thickened, reduced plus as sour cream (either full fat, reduced or light). UHT and aerosol varieties are also available.

Cream is a luxurious food. Pour it into coffee, sauces or over hot or cold desserts. Whip it and fold it through chilled desserts. Blend it into custards, soups or make the quickest mouthwatering sauces by swirling cream into seasonings or pan juices. It also has the ability to soften flavours — even if you think you have ruined a dish, a splash of cream can soften flavours without masking the true flavour of the dish. Whipped cream is also a beautiful garnish when dolloped or piped onto desserts and cakes. Always ensure cream is well chilled before attempting to whip. Once it holds its shape, stop beating or you may end up with a curdled mess!

CHEESE

Cheese is made from the solids that form during the ageing of milk — a rapid process seen by the rate at which fresh milk sours. Cheese-making is a way of controlling this process, by producing a product that is capable of maturing instead of merely spoiling. The craft of cheese-making originated in Europe. Cheeses vary between countries due to climate and milk. These contribute to give a distinctive character to the cheese.

These days we can indulge in cheese even if we are trying to stick to a low fat diet with low fat (less than 15% fat) and reduced fat (75% to 85% fat) varieties now readily available in supermarkets. Low salt varieties are also available. Cheese is an excellent source of top-grade protein, and calcium.

CHEESE GROUPS

1 FRESH UNRIPENED High moisture content cheeses, but low in fat, e.g. cottage cheese, ricotta, quark, mascarpone, Neufchatel. Use them in sandwiches, in sweets, dips, pasta, salads, flans.

2 STRETCH CURD Smooth, close-textured cheeses, e.g. mozzarella and provolone. Others in this group, but matured in brine, are fetta and haloumy. Use them in salads, pizzas, appetisers.

3 CHEDDARS Originating from the English village of Cheddar, this is one of the most popular and versatile cheeses. The cheese is firm, close-textured and light yellow with a delicate to full/strong flavour, depending on its maturity. Some examples are mild, semi-mild, matured (tasty), vintage, processed (which is of a soft texture and lighter colour) e.g. Cheshire, Colby and Leicester. They are great in sandwiches, melted on toast used, as a topping, in salads, soufflés, pies, omelettes, sauces and so on.

4 MOULD UNRIPENED

• White mould, surface ripening cheese, e.g. Brie and Camembert. The ripening process begins at the surface and continues to the centre. It is 'ripe' and ready to eat when the centre is very soft or 'flowing'. Great in salads, cheeseboards, soufflés, pies, etc.

• Blue-veined cheeses. These have a characteristic strong, rich, tangy flavour. Try them in sauces, salad dressings, soufflés, cheeseboards.

5 HARD Parmesan, Romano, pecorino and pepato all belong to this group. They have a low moisture content which makes them perfect for grating. It also helps to increase their shelf life and gives them a distinctive, strong flavour. Great for toppings, pizzas, pasta, coatings and so on.

6 ROUND EYE This category is characterised by cheeses with varying sized 'eyes', e.g. Swiss, Gouda and Edam. They are also of medium fat content. Great for toppings, soufflés, sandwiches, salads and fondues.

CHEESEBOARDS — THE DESSERT ALTERNATIVE

• Prepare a cheeseboard of cheeses that are different in flavour and texture. Simply select one soft cheese, one blue and one harder cheese. Look for contrasts in colour, flavour and texture.

• Serve cheese at room temperature to appreciate the full flavour of the cheese. Remove cheese from refrigerator an hour before serving. Choose a platter or basket and try to provide a separate knife for each type of cheese. Fruit (e.g. strawberries, grapes) and vine leaves make a pretty garnish.

• Complement the cheese with crackers (try a digestive or wheatmeal biscuit with blue cheese), thinly sliced bread, vegetable sticks, fruit or dried fruit and nuts.

• Allow 20 to 30 g of each cheese per person. Delicatessens and specialty shops allow you to purchase specific amounts, while wholesalers allow you to purchase cheaper, bulk amounts.

CALCIUM

Calcium is essential for strengthening our bones and teeth, as well as regulating muscle function, normal clotting of blood, regulation of hormone secretions and activation of enzymes.

Increased calcium is needed during pregnancy and lactation to cover the needs of the mother and baby, for young children to meet the demands of constant bone growth and development and for adolescents who have sudden growth spurts. As men and women age, calcium is lost from the skeleton, with women losing about twice as much as men. Calcium needs to be topped up daily as it is continually being removed from the bones and returned to the bones in a process called remodelling. This ensures that bones grow more dense through childhood and early adulthood. Bones reach their peak strength (called Peak Bone Mass) by about 18 to 20 years with a great increase in strength during adolescence.

OSTEOPOROSIS

Osteoporosis is a condition in which the bones lose calcium, become fragile and vulnerable to fracture. Osteoporosis usually affects people over the age of 40, mostly women. Menopausal hormonal changes accelerate the loss of calcium in the skeleton.

The most important factors in the development of osteoporosis are peak bone mass and the rate of calcium loss from bones. Bones start to lose calcium at about 35 years of age. Around menopause, for 5 to 10 years, women lose bone at a much faster rate than men. This is due to the sharp decline in oestrogen which plays a major role in maintaining bone balance in women.

WHO IS MOST AT RISK?

• The older a person, the more likely osteoporosis is to develop.
• Those who have a family history of osteoporosis.
• Caucasian and Asian women who are slim and have small bones.
• Women after menopause.
• Women who have restricted dietary intake of calcium over long periods of time.
• Those who have a high intake of alcohol, salt and caffeine drinks.
• Those who do very little exercise (excercise increases bone mass).

PREVENTING OSTEOPOROSIS

Some risk factors cannot be altered but certain measures can help to increase or maintain the strength of bones:
• Maintain an adequate dietary intake of calcium — those on restricted diets should consult a doctor or dietician.
• Participate in a variety of sports and regular exercise.
• Moderate intake of alcohol, salt and caffeine and avoid smoking.
• Seek medical advice at time of menopause, and if appropriate, have hormone replacement therapy. (Talk to your doctor or contact a Women's Health Care Centre or Menopause Clinic).

FOOD SOURCES OF CALCIUM

Seventy percent of dietary calcium is supplied by dairy foods (milk, cheese, yoghurt etc) with the remaining 30 percent supplied by grains, vegetables and canned fish (if bones are eaten). Dairy foods contain nutrients which make calcium more readily absorbable than from cereals and vegetables. Check the recommended calcium intake chart as a guide to see if you are getting enough calcium daily.

RECOMMENDED DIETARY INTAKE OF CALCIUM PER DAY

Women	19-54	800 mg		Children	1–7	700–800 mg
Pregnant women (3rd trimester)		1000 mg		Girls	12–15	1000 mg
					16–18	800 mg
Lactating women		1200 mg		Boys	12–15	1200 mg
Women after menopause		1000 mg			16–18	1000 mg
Infants	0–1	300–550 mg		Men	19–64+	800 mg

(Source: Recommended dietary intakes for use in Australia NHMRC 1991.)

AVERAGE CALCIUM CONTENT OF A VARIETY OF FOODS

SERVE SIZE	CALCIUM (MG)	SERVE SIZE	CALCIUM (MG)
1 cup (250 ml) full cream milk	295	100 g low fat cottage cheese	75
1 cup (250 ml) skim milk	320	1 slice bread (white or wholegrain)	20
1 cup (250 ml) modified, reduced fat milk	355	1 cup cooked spinach	170
1 cup (250 ml) modified low fat milk	415	1 cup cooked broccoli	30
1 cup (200 g) natural yoghurt	340	½ cup cooked green beans	35
1 cup (200 g) low fat natural yoghurt	420	½ cup cooked kidney beans	30
1 cup (200 g) reduced fat fruit yoghurt	320	¾ cup canned salmon	160
35 g Cheddar cheese	270	50 g canned sardines (including bones)	150
35 g reduced fat Edam cheese	360	15 almonds	50

Dairy Food *with* FRUIT

Yoghurt, cream, butter, milk and cheese are an integral part of good cooking and healthy eating. Choose low-fat varieties if you prefer: the taste is still sensational.

Fruit and dairy products are an unbeatable combination for creating salads or starters, drinks or desserts. Both sweet and savoury dishes are given here: try a delicious dressing for a fruity salad or a refreshing fruit drink; choose from ice cream, custards and simple fruit salads. The result is always refreshing and inviting.

The simplicity of cheese and fruit makes a wonderful end to any meal or even a quick, healthy snack. With a little imagination, the choices are limitless.

*Tangy Mango
Yoghurt Salad*

TANGY MANGO YOGHURT SALAD ⚖

1 cup (200 g) natural yoghurt

1 teaspoon wholegrain mustard

**1 green chilli, very finely chopped or
cayenne pepper, to taste**

1 tablespoon desiccated coconut

salt

1 large mango, diced

2 spring onions, chopped

1 Beat yoghurt in a bowl until smooth.
2 Add mustard, chilli, coconut and salt to
taste.
3 Stir in the mango and spring onions.
Serve chilled.

SERVES 4 TO 6

❦ **YOGHURT**

*Yoghurt will keep in the
refrigerator for 7 to
10 days. Always check
the use-by date. Yoghurt
cannot be frozen.
If heating yoghurt in a
recipe, take care not
to boil it as it will curdle
or separate.*

TURKEY, HAM *and* COTTAGE CHEESE SALAD ⚖

8 lettuce leaves

8 slices cooked turkey

8 slices ham

2 to 3 peaches, peeled and sliced

½ cup (100 g) cottage cheese

3 nectarines, halved and seeded

1 capsicum (pepper), sliced

alfalfa sprouts, to garnish

1 Tear the lettuce leaves into bite-sized
pieces and place on a large platter.
2 Alternately layer turkey, ham and peach
slices on lettuce leaves.
3 Fill stone cavity of nectarines with a
teaspoonful of cottage cheese. Place
nectarines decoratively on platter, arrange
capsicum slices on top and sprinkle over the
alfalfa sprouts.

SERVES 6

PRAWN *and* PAWPAW SALAD *with* CITRUS MAYONNAISE

1 kg pawpaw

1 lemon

1 orange

¾ cup (180 ml) mayonnaise

3 tablespoons cream

2 tablespoons chopped fresh dill

750 g cooked prawns (shrimps), shelled and deveined

freshly ground black pepper

fresh dill sprigs, to garnish

1 Halve pawpaw, scoop out seeds, peel and cut into slices lengthways.

2 Carefully peel rind only of lemon and orange. Cut into julienne strips, blanch in boiling water for 5 minutes, drain, refresh and reserve for garnishing. Squeeze the juice of both fruits.

3 Combine mayonnaise with lemon and orange juice to taste. Whip cream until thickened and soft peaks form then gently fold into mayonnaise with dill.

4 Arrange the pawpaw slices and prawns on a serving plate, season with pepper then spoon over mayonnaise. Garnish with fresh dill sprigs and orange and lemon rind.

SERVES 6

CITRUS FRUIT

Obtain extra juice from citrus fruit by heating in your microwave oven on HIGH for 30 seconds before squeezing.

When grating skin from citrus fruits, use a fine grater and only remove the colour of the skin — the white pith is bitter.

Prawn and Pawpaw Salad with Citrus Mayonnaise

FRUITY COLESLAW *with* COTTAGE CHEESE ⚖

½ pineapple, halved lengthways

1 cup shredded cabbage

2 stalks celery, chopped

1 large orange, peeled and segmented

1 bunch grapes

½ cup (100 g) creamed cottage cheese

freshly ground black pepper

3 tablespoons chopped fresh mint

1 Scoop out pineapple from shell leaving shell intact and dice pineapple flesh.

2 Combine diced pineapple, cabbage, celery, orange and grapes.

3 Season cottage cheese with pepper and mint. Toss through salad. Spoon back into pineapple shell and serve.

SERVES 4

CREAM CHEESE *and* MANGO

250 g fresh ricotta cheese

1 teaspoon vanilla essence

4 tablespoons Marsala

½ cup (125 ml) cream

2 egg whites

3 tablespoons caster sugar

grated chocolate or chocolate curls, to garnish

1 mango, cut into 6 slices

1 In a blender combine ricotta, vanilla essence, Marsala and cream. Blend for 30 seconds or until ingredients are smooth.

2 Whisk egg whites until stiff, then gradually add sugar. Fold through ricotta mixture.

3 Spoon onto dessert plates and sprinkle with grated chocolate. Arrange a mango slice alongside.

SERVES 6

BANANA YOGHURT MUNCH ⚖

1 banana, sliced

1 tablespoon fresh lemon juice

1 large mango, diced

¾ cup (90 g) granola cereal or toasted muesli

1 cup (200 g) natural yoghurt

1 Sprinkle lemon juice over banana slices.

2 Divide mango between two serving dishes. Sprinkle with a little granola and cover with half the yoghurt.

3 Spoon banana into dishes, cover with remaining yoghurt and top with remaining granola.

SERVES 2

TROPICAL FRUIT SALAD *with* MANGO CREAM

FRUIT SALAD

2 mangoes, sliced

½ small pineapple, cubed

2 kiwi fruit, sliced

250 g punnet strawberries, hulled

½ cup (45 g) walnuts

4 tablespoons Cointreau or orange juice

2 passionfruit, to garnish

MANGO CREAM

1 mango, puréed

¾ cup (180 ml) cream, whipped

1 TO PREPARE SALAD: Put fruit and nuts into a large bowl or six individual serving dishes. Pour over Cointreau and refrigerate for 1 to 2 hours.

2 TO PREPARE MANGO CREAM: Fold mango purée through firmly whipped cream.

3 Serve fruit salad with mango cream, garnished with passionfruit.

SERVES 6

CRÊPES NINETTE

The batter may be prepared and crêpes made the day before. They may be stored, frozen, between greased paper in stacks of six.

BATTER
1 cup (125 g) plain flour
pinch salt
2 eggs
⅔ cup (160 ml) milk
⅔ cup (160 ml) water
2 tablespoons butter, melted
vanilla essence

FILLING
125 g butter
½ cup (155 g) honey
3 tablespoons sugar
4 sweet apples, peeled, cored and sliced

TO SERVE
2 tablespoons caster sugar
juice 1 lemon
4 tablespoons Grand Marnier

1 TO PREPARE BATTER: Sift flour and salt into bowl. Blend in eggs and beat in combined milk, water and melted butter a little at a time, to form a smooth batter. Stir in vanilla essence to taste, and rest batter for 1 hour.

2 Grease heated crêpe pan with butter and pour enough batter into pan to coat base, making an even circle. Cook over moderate heat until brown. Turn crêpe and brown other side, remove from pan and keep warm. Repeat procedure until batter is finished.

3 TO PREPARE FILLING: Melt butter in a pan, add honey and sugar and stir until sugar melts. Add apple slices and cook gently until soft. Strain apple from pan and use to fill crêpes.

4 Return filled crêpes to pan and heat gently, basting often with the syrup. Sprinkle with caster sugar and lemon juice.

5 Heat Grand Marnier in a small saucepan, ignite with a taper and pour over crêpes in pan. Serve at once. This final step can be done at the last minute and brought to the table in front of the guests.

MAKES 6

Crêpes Ninette

 CRÊPE BATTER

Crêpe batter should be the consistency of pouring cream. Add extra liquid until you achieve this consistency.

Step-by-Step Techniques

Whisk egg whites in a bain marie until stiff.

Fold in strawberry purée.

Place in prepared soufflé dish and freeze.

Iced Strawberry Soufflé

An iced soufflé should resemble a baked soufflé. To achieve this, create a collar around the dish, using non-stick baking paper. The collar should stand approximately 5 cm above the dish. Do not beat after placing in the freezer!

¾ cup (185 g) sugar

½ cup (125 ml) water

3 egg whites

1¼ cups (300 ml) cream, whipped and chilled

fresh lemon juice, to taste

500 g strawberries, cleaned, hulled and puréed

1 In a pan, dissolve sugar in water, bring to the boil and boil for 5 minutes.

2 Whisk egg whites in a bain marie or double boiler until stiff. Pour hot sugar syrup onto egg whites slowly, whisking constantly. Remove from heat, whisk to cool.

3 Fold in cream, lemon juice and strawberry purée. Place mixture in a serving container and freeze.

MAKES 1 LITRE

❦ EGG YOLKS

Leftover egg yolks can be used to bind dishes, emulsify ingredients in dressings (such as mayonnaise), thicken and enrich a sauce, and make pastry.

FRESH FRUIT CRUSH ⚖

Other soft fruits can be substituted such as raspberries, apricots or ripe pears.

1¼ cups (300 ml) skim milk
250 g strawberries, washed and hulled
1 banana, sliced
1 mango, peeled, stoned and sliced
3 tablespoons fresh mint leaves
1 cup crushed ice

1 Place all ingredients in a blender and blend until smooth.

SERVES 4

CITRUS YOGHURT DELIGHT ⚖

40 g butter
juice 2 lemons
3 to 4 tablespoons brown sugar
¼ teaspoon cinnamon
2 apples, sliced into wedges
2 bananas, sliced
1 cup (200 g) low fat natural yoghurt

1 Place butter, lemon juice, sugar and cinnamon into a frying pan. Heat until butter melts and add apples and bananas. Cook for 1 to 2 minutes on each side.
2 Serve with yoghurt, or as an alternative, poured over ice cream.

SERVES 4

APRICOT YOGHURT RICE CREAM ⚖

Any flavoured yoghurt and fruit may be used for this nutritious and low fat recipe.

1 cup (185 g) short grain rice
3 cups (750 ml) low fat milk
1 cup (200 g) low fat apricot yoghurt
425 g canned unsweetened apricots, drained
ground nutmeg

1 In a saucepan, bring rice and milk to the boil, then simmer for 15 to 20 minutes until rice is cooked and liquid absorbed, stirring occasionally.
2 Stir in yoghurt and apricots, heat gently.
3 Sprinkle with nutmeg to serve.

SERVES 6

FROZEN FRUIT MOUSSE

Any fruit in season can be used such as mangoes, peaches, pears or apricots. Liqueur can be added if desired.

4 egg yolks
1½ cups (375 g) sugar
2 cups prepared fruit, puréed
1 to 2 cups (250 ml to 500 ml) whipped cream

1 Whip sugar and egg yolks together over a bain-marie until thick. Add to fruit pulp in food processor and blend.
2 Add whipped cream and blend in short bursts for 2 to 3 seconds. Freeze in trays for 1 to 1½ hours.

SERVES 4

HEATING YOGHURT

Stir yoghurt through hot dishes gently and just before serving, to prevent curdling. Heat yoghurt very gently.

WHIPPING CREAM

Always ensure that cream is cold before attempting to whip it. After opening, cream keeps for about 5 days in the refrigerator.

APPLE DELICIOUS

Low in fat but high in flavour, low fat ricotta cheese can be subsituted for cottage cheese.

APPLE DELICIOUS

30 g butter

⅓ cup (90 g) sugar

3 tablespoons self-raising flour

⅓ cup (80 ml) skim milk

1 cup (200 g) low fat creamed cottage cheese

2 to 3 apples, stewed

⅓ cup (60 g) currants

rind 1 lemon, grated

2 eggs, separated

1 Preheat oven to 180°C (350°F).

2 In a bowl, cream butter and sugar. Add flour, mixing well.

3 Stir in remaining ingredients except egg whites.

4 Whip egg whites until stiff. Fold through apple mixture.

5 Pour into an 18 cm round casserole dish. Bake for 45 minutes until set and golden brown on top.

SERVES 5

YOGHURT LEMON DRESSING

Mix 1 cup yoghurt with some finely grated lemon rind and 3 tablespoons fresh lemon juice. Add 2 tablespoons freshly chopped mint and 2 tablespoons honey. Mix well, cover and refrigerate overnight.

BRISK BANANA WHISK

Using low fat dairy products this drink is healthy, low in fat and high in calcium.

1 banana, roughly sliced

2 tablespoons reduced fat natural yoghurt

1 teaspoon honey

1 cup (250 ml) reduced fat milk

2 teaspoons wheatgerm

pinch cinnamon

1 Place all ingredients except cinnamon in a blender and purée till smooth.

2 Pour into a glass and sprinkle with cinnamon.

SERVES 1

GINGERED YOGHURT PEARS

4 ripe pears, peeled, halved and cored

fresh lemon juice

1 cup (200 g) low fat natural yoghurt

rind ½ lemon, finely grated

1 tablespoon finely chopped glacé ginger

1 small ripe pear, peeled, cored and pressed through a sieve

pinch cayenne pepper

1 Sprinkle pears with a little lemon juice to prevent browning.

2 Place hollow side down into four individual serving dishes.

3 Combine remaining ingredients and pour over pears.

SERVES 4

FRUIT *with* MINT *and* YOGHURT

¼ small sugar melon, cut into chunks

½ pineapple, chopped

3 peaches, sliced

3 nectarines, sliced

4 kiwi fruit, sliced

250 g punnet strawberries, hulled and halved

2 bananas, sliced

juice 1 lemon

2 tablespoons caster sugar

6 tablespoons chopped fresh mint

yoghurt or cream, to serve

1 Prepare fruit. Pour lemon juice over fruit and sprinkle over caster sugar. Garnish with mint. Refrigerate until ready to serve. Serve with natural yoghurt, or Yoghurt Lemon Dressing (see recipe) or whipped cream.

SERVES 6

Fruit with Mint and Yoghurt

ICE CREAM STRAWBERRY WHIP

2 mangoes, chopped

1 cup (250 ml) milk

1 tablespoon maple syrup

3 drops almond essence

2 cups (400 g) strawberry ice cream

1 Combine first four ingredients and blend until smooth.

2 Add ice cream and blend for 10 seconds more. Serve immediately.

SERVES 4 TO 6

*Ice Cream
Strawberry Whip*

BAKED APPLE *and* SAGO PUDDING

**2½ cups (625 ml) milk
(or low fat or reduced fat milk)**

¼ cup (30 g) sago

3 eggs

2 tablespoons honey

pinch ground nutmeg

pinch ground cloves

2 apples peeled, cored and sliced

30 g butter

1 Preheat oven to 180°C (350°F).

2 In a pan bring milk and sago to the boil and cook for 8 minutes. Leave to cool.

3 Beat in eggs, honey and spices.

4 In another pan, gently cook apples in butter until soft. Arrange in a soufflé dish and top with sago mixture. Place dish in a baking tray half filled with hot water and bake for 45 minutes. Serve cold.

SERVES 4

APPLE, BERRY *and* BUTTERMILK PANCAKES

BATTER

1 cup (125 g) self-raising flour

1 tablespoon caster sugar

1 egg

¾ to 1 cup (180 ml to 250 ml) cultured buttermilk

1 apple, grated

250 g punnet strawberries, or any berry in season

CUSTARD SAUCE

3 tablespoons custard powder

2 cups (500 ml) skim milk or buttermilk

liquid sweetener or sugar

1 To Prepare Batter: Sift flour and sugar into a bowl. Lightly beat egg and make up to 1 cup (250 ml) with buttermilk. Stir into flour until smooth. Stir through grated apple.

2 Drop large spoonfuls of batter into a hot non-stick frypan. Flatten out slightly. When golden brown on the bottom and bubbles appear on the surface, turn over and cook until browned. Set aside and keep warm while making remaining pancakes.

3 To Prepare Custard Sauce: Mix custard powder with a little milk to form a smooth paste. Heat remaining milk in a saucepan. Add custard powder and stir until thickened. Add liquid sweetener to taste.

4 Serve hot with berries on top and hot custard sauce poured over.

SERVES 8

COLD CITRUS CHIFFON

6 eggs, separated

¾ cup (185 g) sugar

1½ cups (375 ml) fresh orange juice

2 tablespoons fresh lemon juice

2½ tablespoons powdered gelatine softened in ½ cup (125 ml) orange juice and dissolved over hot water

1 teaspoon grated lemon rind

2 tablespoons grated orange rind

½ teaspoon orange liqueur

3 tablespoons sugar, extra

2½ cups (625 ml) cream, whipped

GARNISH

1¼ cups (310 ml) extra cream for decoration or to serve separately (optional)

8 orange segments

shredded rind 1 orange

1 Lightly butter a 7 cup (1.7 litre) soufflé dish. Prepare a greaseproof collar to fit around and extend 8 cm above the rim. Lightly butter, tie and tape securely in position.

2 Beat egg yolks and sugar in a bowl for 10 minutes or until mousse-like. Add orange and lemon juices gradually. Stir in dissolved gelatine. Add lemon and orange rinds and liqueur. Cool in refrigerator until mixture is a soft gel-like consistency. Do not allow it to set. Remove bowl and let rise to room temperature.

3 Whip egg whites until soft peaks form and beat in the extra sugar gradually until of meringue consistency. Fold egg whites and cream into the orange mixture alternately. Pour into soufflé dish and refrigerate for 3 hours until set.

4 Before serving, remove paper collar from around soufflé dish. Whip extra cream and pipe on top of soufflé. Decorate with orange segments and shredded orange rind.

SERVES 6 TO 8

Cold Citrus Chiffon

 BUTTERMILK

Use buttermilk within a few days of opening, though it can be stored unopened for a couple of weeks.

Dairy Food *with* VEGETABLES

Far from being an afterthought, vegetables can be the central focus of a meal, the basis for soups, salads and hearty main courses.

So many vegetable dishes rely on cheese, butter, cream, yoghurt and milk for their appeal: potatoes with a cheesy filling, for instance, or broccoli with a cream sauce. These are winning combinations in the nutrition stakes, rich in fibre, vitamins and calcium.

The recipes in this chapter reflect the many ways vegetables can be used. Wrap them in filo, thread them onto kebabs, toss them in a tangy dressing or bake them in mouthwatering mixtures with crispy cheese toppings. Whatever your choice, you'll love the results.

SALAD
DRESSING

*Never dress salad until
ready to serve, unless
otherwise instructed.*

 SOME SALAD
DRESSING IDEAS

*Process 1 cup (250 ml)
sour cream, 125 g
crumbled blue vein cheese,
lemon juice and Tabasco
sauce and seasonings
to taste for a quick
and delicious blue
vein dressing.
For a great low kilojoule
dressing, combine cottage
cheese, lemon juice or
vinegar and seasonings,
with a dash of curry
powder or chutney for
added flavour.*

COLESLAW *with* BUTTERMILK DRESSING ⚖

**1 large green apple, cut into thin sticks
with skin on**

fresh lemon juice

½ red cabbage, shredded

1 carrot, grated

⅓ cup (60 g) sultanas

BUTTERMILK DRESSING

½ red capsicum (pepper), roughly chopped

1 stalk celery, roughly chopped

1 onion, roughly chopped

¾ cup (180 ml) buttermilk

1 Sprinkle lemon juice over apple to
prevent browning. Toss salad ingredients
together in a bowl.

2 TO PREPARE BUTTERMILK DRESSING:
Blend all ingredients in a food processor
until smooth. Season to taste then chill.

3 Pour dressing over salad. Cover and chill.

SERVES 4 TO 6

CREAM OF AVOCADO SOUP

40 g butter

1 onion, thinly sliced

1 stalk celery, chopped

2 tablespoons plain flour

2 cups (500 ml) vegetable stock

1 tablespoon fresh lemon juice

1 tablespoon horseradish

1 clove garlic, crushed

1 teaspoon curry powder

salt and freshly ground black pepper

pinch tarragon and allspice

1 avocado, peeled and mashed

1 cup (250 ml) milk

1 cup (250 ml) cream

1 In a saucepan, melt butter and sauté
onion and celery until tender. Stir in
flour. Make a roux, stir in stock and cook
until smooth.

2 Add lemon juice, horseradish, garlic,
curry powder and salt. Simmer for
5 minutes. Dust lightly with pepper,
tarragon and allspice.

3 Stir a little soup into the avocado then
add to soup and mix well until smooth.
Stir in milk and cream and heat through but
do not boil.

SERVES 6

GOUDA GARDEN SALAD

1 lettuce

**100 g Gouda, cut into 1 cm x 3 cm sticks
(reduced fat Gouda or Edam can be used)**

1 cucumber, sliced

250 g strawberries, hulled

1 mandarin, segmented

1 pear, sliced

100 g snow peas (mangetout), blanched

DRESSING

grated rind 1 lemon

¼ cup (60 ml) prepared French dressing

1 clove garlic, crushed

1 Combine salad ingredients.

2 TO PREPARE DRESSING: Blend lemon
rind with dressing and garlic. Shake well
and pour over salad.

SERVES 4 TO 6

SPINACH *and* EDAM SALAD ⚖

275 g spinach

175 g reduced fat Edam cheese, diced

2 carrots, cut into strips

1 red capsicum (pepper), cut into strips

2 spring onions, sliced

4 radishes, sliced

75 g button mushrooms, sliced

3 tablespoons raisins

juice 1 orange

juice 1 lemon

1 Tear spinach leaves into pieces and place with all other ingredients, except juices, in a salad bowl.

2 Combine orange and lemon juice, pour over salad and toss lightly.

SERVES 4

GREEN SALAD *with* BLUE CHEESE DRESSING

75 g blue-veined cheese

1 cup (250 ml) cream (reduced fat cream can be used)

pinch cayenne pepper

2 teaspoons finely chopped chives

2 soft lettuces

1 Blend together cheese and cream until soft then push through a sieve to remove any lumps. Season with pepper and gently stir in the chives.

2 Wash lettuce, remove the cores and separate into leaves. Place in a salad bowl and pour over the cheese dressing. Serve immediately.

SERVES 6

Green Salad with Blue Cheese Dressing

🧀 CHEESY FACTS

• *Hasten the ripening of soft cheeses by leaving them at room temperature.*

• *Cheese is great with salads, sandwiches, crispbread and fruit for a healthy meal or snack.*

• *If fresh cheeses such as cottage cheese or ricotta are used, then the kilojoule count is even lower.*

Nutty Yoghurt Salad

CREAMY EGGPLANT DIP ⚖

1 large eggplant (aubergine)

1 onion, chopped

1 clove garlic, crushed

1 tablespoon chopped fresh parsley

juice ½ lemon

**250 g cream cheese
(reduced fat cream cheese can be used)**

1 Prick eggplant with fork and bake at 190°C (375°F) for 45 minutes, until very soft. Cool then cut in half and scoop out flesh.

2 Blend flesh with remaining ingredients and season to taste.

3 Serve in a dip bowl with vegetable sticks.

SERVES 6

NUTTY YOGHURT SALAD

1 bunch silverbeet, blanched and shredded

1 cucumber, sliced

⅓ cup (40 g) pecan nuts, lightly toasted

1 bunch spring onions, chopped

12 stalks asparagus, blanched

½ cup (100 g) natural yoghurt

1 clove garlic, crushed

1 Toss together silverbeet, cucumber, pecans, spring onions and asparagus.
2 Combine yoghurt and garlic and mix well. Pour over salad.

SERVES 4

VEGETABLE KEBABS *with* RICOTTA ⚖

Any fresh vegetables in season may be used, e.g. baby squash, carrot, potato, broccoli, brussels sprouts.

2 zucchini (courgettes), thickly sliced

12 button mushrooms

½ cauliflower, broken into florets

425 g canned baby corn, drained (optional)

1 red capsicum (pepper), cut into 3 cm squares

RICOTTA SAUCE

200 g smooth ricotta cheese

425 g canned tomato purée

1 onion, finely chopped

1 clove garlic, crushed

½ teaspoon mixed herbs

1 Thread vegetables alternately onto 12 skewers. Serve raw or steam the kebabs for 10 minutes.

2 TO PREPARE SAUCE: Place all ingredients in a saucepan. Heat gently to simmering point, cook for 10 minutes, stirring occasionally.

3 Serve kebabs with sauce poured over.

SERVES 6

CREAMY POTATO BAKE

1 kg potatoes, peeled

1 clove garlic, crushed

100 g butter, softened

CHEESE MIXTURE

2 eggs

2½ cups (625 ml) milk

¾ cup (180 ml) cream

salt and freshly ground black pepper

grated nutmeg

125 g Gruyère cheese, grated

1 Preheat oven to 200°C (400°F).

2 Place potatoes in a saucepan of salted water and bring to the boil. Boil for 1 minute, then drain, cool slightly and thinly slice.

3 Rub garlic around the inside of an ovenproof dish. Use half the butter to grease the dish.

4 TO PREPARE CHEESE MIXTURE: Whisk eggs, milk, cream, salt, pepper and nutmeg together in a bowl and beat. Stir in half the cheese.

5 Cover bottom of greased dish with a layer of potato slices. Cover with a little cheese mixture. Continue with alternate layers of potato and cheese mixture until both are all used. Sprinkle top with remaining grated cheese and dot with butter.

6 Bake in oven for 45 minutes. Cover with foil if it becomes too brown. Serve with roast meat or grilled steak.

SERVES 4

CHEESY STUFFED POTATOES ⚖

6 large potatoes

200 g pumpkin, cooked

1 cup (200 g) low fat creamed cottage cheese

4 spring onions, chopped

¼ teaspoon ground nutmeg

salt and freshly ground black pepper

1 Bake potatoes in their skins for 1 hour at 180°C (350°F) or until cooked.

2 Cut tops off, scoop out flesh leaving a thin layer of potato around the skin.

3 Mash pumpkin with potato. Add remaining ingredients, mix well, season to taste. Spoon potato mixture back into shells. Cook for 15 minutes in the oven.

SERVES 6

 CREAMY POTATO BAKE

For a delicious variation, add layers of sautéed, sliced mushrooms and chopped onions. Never use raw potatoes in this dish — very often they will cause the milk to curdle. Parboiling the potatoes first or thickening the milk with cornflour (cornstarch) will prevent this.

GRATED CHEESE

Use a fine grater for hard cheeses and a coarse grater for softer ones. Store left over grated cheese in an airtight container in the refrigerator or in well sealed freezer bags.

STEP-BY-STEP TECHNIQUES

SPINACH *and* CHEESE TURNOVERS

500 g puff pastry

1 egg, beaten

1 tablespoon sesame seeds

FILLING

750 g frozen spinach, thawed

90 g Cheddar cheese, grated

pinch ground nutmeg

salt and freshly ground black pepper

2 egg yolks, beaten

juice 1 lemon

1 Preheat oven to 200°C (400°F).

2 Roll out pastry 3 mm thick. Using a round pastry cutter, cut out circles 10 cm in diameter.

3 TO PREPARE FILLING: Drain spinach and squeeze to extract as much water as possible, then chop finely. Place in a bowl with cheese, nutmeg, seasoning, egg yolks and lemon juice. Mix well.

4 Divide filling between pastry circles. Brush edges of pastry with water. Fold pastry over spinach and press edges together firmly. Brush pastry circles with beaten egg and sprinkle with sesame seeds.

5 Place turnovers on a greased baking tray and bake for 20 minutes.

SERVES 4

Place spinach mixture on pastry circles.

Fold over pastry edges and press together firmly.

Brush with egg and sprinkle with sesame seeds.

TOMATOES ROQUEFORT

4 tomatoes, thinly sliced

1 onion, thinly sliced into rings

1 tablespoon chopped fresh parsley

125 g Roquefort cheese

2 tablespoons olive oil

2 tablespoons fresh lemon juice

1 teaspoon sugar

freshly ground black pepper

pinch paprika

1 Place tomatoes on a serving dish and cover with a layer of onion rings.

2 Blend all remaining ingredients until creamy and pour over tomato/onion base. Chill before serving.

SERVES 4

CHEESY SOUFFLÉ POTATOES

4 large old potatoes, washed

1 cup (125 g) grated Cheddar cheese

freshly ground black pepper

4 tablespoons sour cream

1 tablespoon chopped chives

1 tablespoon chopped fresh parsley

pinch paprika

2 egg yolks

3 egg whites

1 Preheat oven to 180°C (350°F).

2 Pierce potatoes with a skewer in several places and bake for 1 to 1½ hours. The potatoes should be cooked but still intact. Cut a lid off each potato and scoop out the centre, leaving some of the flesh around the skin to form a casing.

3 Mash the potato with all remaining ingredients except egg whites.

4 Beat egg whites until stiff and gently fold into potato mixture. Spoon into potato cases and place them on an oven tray. Bake in the oven until tops are golden brown and puffy.

SERVES 4

BROCCOLI *in* BUTTERMILK SAUCE

500 g broccoli

1 cup (250 ml) buttermilk

2 tablespoons cornflour

1 cup (200 g) yoghurt

freshly ground black pepper

2 teaspoons chopped capers

½ teaspoon turmeric

4 tablespoons sour cream

1 Trim broccoli stalks and slit from base to flower. Peel stalks if they look woody. Stand stalks in boiling salted water with the flower heads above the water and cook for about 8 minutes, until stalks are tender. Drain and cover to keep warm while preparing sauce.

2 Blend buttermilk with cornflour and heat in a saucepan, stirring occasionally. Add yoghurt, pepper, capers and turmeric, stirring until sauce thickens.

3 Add sour cream and heat through without boiling.

4 Place broccoli on a serving dish, spoon some sauce over and serve the remainder separately.

SERVES 4

CHOPPING ONIONS

To avoid tears when chopping onions, leave the root end intact. This will also make chopping easier. Running the chopped end under cold water will reduce odour.

FOLDING EGG WHITES

Always fold beaten egg whites into a mixture gently with a metal spoon or other sharp edge utensil (spatula) to help prevent air being lost. Never BEAT egg whites into a mixture.

VEGETABLE CRUMBLE ⚖

250 g spinach, stalks removed

2 carrots, sliced

1 large zucchini (courgette), sliced

1 large onion, sliced

200 g cauliflower florets

90 g cabbage, shredded

25 g butter

1 tablespoon plain flour

3 cups (750 ml) skim milk

175 g Edam or Gouda cheese, finely grated (reduced fat Edam or Gouda can be used)

2 teaspoons curry powder

salt and freshly ground black pepper

2 slices bread, crumbed

1 Preheat oven to 190°C (375°F).

2 Cook spinach, covered, in a little water for 10 minutes.

Vegetable Crumble

Place vegetables in ovenproof dish.

Pour sauce over vegetables.

3 Place carrots, zucchini, onion, cauliflower and cabbage in a saucepan and barely cover with water. Bring to the boil, then drain, reserving ⅔ cup (160 ml) of the liquid.

4 Place vegetables in an ovenproof dish and arrange spinach on top. Melt butter, stir in flour and cook for 1 minute.

5 Gradually stir in reserved vegetable liquid and milk. Bring to the boil and simmer for 2 minutes, stirring continuously.

6 Stir in 100 g of the cheese, curry powder and season to taste. Spoon over the vegetables. Combine remaining cheese with breadcrumbs and sprinkle over vegetables. Bake in oven for 30 minutes. Serve hot.

SERVES 4

EGGPLANT AND WALNUT PUFF

500 g eggplant (aubergine)

40 g butter

2 tablespoons plain flour

1 cup (250 ml) milk

4 eggs, separated

2 tablespoons chopped walnuts

pinch grated nutmeg

freshly ground black pepper

1 Bake eggplant whole at 200°C (400°F) for 30 minutes or until pulp is soft.

2 Melt butter in a pan, stir in flour and cook for 1 minute. Gradually add milk, stirring continuously until thick and smooth. Remove sauce from the heat and stir in lightly beaten egg yolks with walnuts, nutmeg and pepper.

3 Split the eggplant, scrape out pulp, mash well and stir it into the sauce. Beat egg whites until stiff and fold them into the sauce.

4 Pour mixture into an oiled soufflé dish and bake at 190°C (375°F) for 45 minutes. Serve immediately.

SERVES 2 TO 4

Cheesy Cabbage Rolls

CHEESY CABBAGE ROLLS

1 cup (185 g) rice

3 tablespoons toasted pine nuts

1 tomato, diced

1 small red capsicum (pepper), chopped

10 fresh basil leaves, chopped

250 g Cheddar cheese, grated

8 cabbage leaves, stalks removed

1 Preheat oven to 180°C (350°F)

2 Cook rice according to instructions on packet. Combine rice with pine nuts, tomato, capsicum, basil and cheese.

3 Blanch cabbage leaves in boiling water for 30 seconds or until limp. Remove from water immediately.

4 Firmly pack equal amounts of filling in the centre of each leaf. Roll up tightly and secure with a toothpick.

5 Place cabbage rolls in the top of a steamer. Steam, over gently simmering water for 5 minutes or until heated through. Alternatively, pour 1 cup (250 ml) tomato purée over rolls in a casserole dish. Bake for 10 to 15 minutes.

MAKES 8 ROLLS

VEGETABLES *in* FILO

300 g vintage Cheddar cheese, grated

8 mushrooms, sliced

200 g broccoli florets

1 large capsicum (pepper), diced

4 spring onions, sliced

pepper

6 sheets filo pastry

sesame or poppy seeds

125 g butter, melted

1 Preheat oven to 190°C (375°F).

2 In a large bowl combine cheese, broccoli, mushrooms, capsicum and spring onions. Season to taste with pepper and mix well.

3 Separate filo pastry sheets, brushing each with melted butter.

4 Spread filling to within 2 cm of the pastry edges. Roll up securely, sealing edges with melted butter. Place sealed side down on a buttered baking tray. Brush with melted butter and sprinkle with sesame seeds. Make two small slits in the parcel then bake for 25 minutes. Serve immediately.

SERVES 4

FILO PASTRY

When using filo pastry, never leave uncovered unless brushed with melted butter. This will prevent drying out of the pastry which makes it almost impossible to handle. Otherwise, cover with a damp tea-towel.

COOKING VEGETABLES

Do not soak vegetables in water as this causes vitamin loss.
When cooking vegetables, chop them in even-sized pieces as large as possible for even cooking and minimum vitamin loss.
If boiling, use only a small amount of water and short cooking times.

DID YOU KNOW?

• *Use gentle heat when cooking cheese or it will become oily and stringy. Excessive baking or grilling can produce a leathery result.*

• *Add finely grated Parmesan cheese to breadcrumbs for delicious stuffings and toppings. Try it in batters, scone doughs and pastries.*

• *When using cheese as a topping, grease the dish so that the cheese doesn't stick to the rim.*

COTTAGE CHEESE VEGETABLE BAKE ⚖

SPINACH MIXTURE

1 tablespoon vegetable oil

2 onions, chopped

2 cloves garlic, chopped

1 bunch spinach, washed and stalks removed

2 cups (400 g) cottage cheese

2 cups (250 g) cooked soy beans

½ cup (60 g) chopped walnuts

½ cup (60 g) sultanas

¼ cup (60 ml) tomato paste (concentrated tomato purée)

1 small carrot, grated

¼ teaspoon fresh dill

salt and freshly ground black pepper

1 tomato, sliced

FRESH TOMATO FILLING

2 tomatoes, peeled and chopped

1 small onion, chopped

1 tablespoon chopped fresh mint

1 tablespoon fresh lemon juice

pinch cayenne

pinch salt

1 Preheat oven to 180°C (350°F).

2 TO PREPARE SPINACH MIXTURE: Heat oil in a frying pan and sauté onions and garlic until soft but not brown.

3 Steam spinach until just tender. Chop finely and drain in a colander. Squeeze spinach to remove all excess liquid.

4 Combine spinach with cooked onion and all remaining ingredients except tomato slices.

5 Grease and line a ring tin. Place tomato slices on base of dish. Cover with spinach mixture and press down firmly.

6 Cover tin with foil and bake for 45 minutes, removing foil after 25 minutes. If not firm after 45 minutes, bake

10 minutes more. Stand for 10 minutes before turning out onto serving plate.

7 TO PREPARE FRESH TOMATO FILLING: Combine all ingredients.

8 Fill centre of vegetable ring with tomato filling and serve.

SERVES 6

RICOTTA NUT TERRINE

1 tablespoon oil

1½ cups (185 g) chopped celery

2 onions, chopped

½ cup (60 g) almond meal

1 cup (125 g) chopped walnuts

1 cup (125 g) toasted, chopped cashew nuts

¼ cup (30 g) rolled oats

1 tablespoon sesame seeds

250 g cottage cheese (ricotta cheese can be used)

3 eggs

¼ teaspoon freshly ground black pepper

1 teaspoon chopped fresh parsley

¼ teaspoon dried marjoram

1 Preheat oven to 180°C (350°F).

2 Heat oil and cook celery and onion until golden. Drain and place in a bowl with all remaining ingredients. Mix thoroughly.

3 Grease two 10 x 20 cm loaf tins, and line with greaseproof paper. Spoon half the mixture into each. Bake for 45 minutes and test for firmness by pressing lightly with your finger. If the terrine is not firm, bake for a further 5 to 8 minutes.

4 Leave to cool slightly in the pan, then turn out onto a plate and remove the paper. Serve hot or cold with a salad.

SERVES 8 TO 10

SAVOURY PANCAKES

PANCAKES

1½ cups (185 g) plain flour, sifted

2 teaspoons mixed herbs

2½ cups (625 ml) skim milk
(buttermilk can be substituted)

1 egg, lightly beaten

FILLING

100 g Cheddar cheese, grated

2 zucchini (courgettes), sliced and blanched

4 silverbeet leaves, shredded and blanched

CHILLI SAUCE

30 g butter

2 cloves garlic, crushed

1 onion, chopped

2 tablespoons plain flour

425 g canned tomato purée

1 to 2 teaspoons chilli sauce or powder

1 cup (250 ml) water

1 teaspoon dried basil

1 Preheat oven to 180°C (350°F).

2 TO PREPARE PANCAKES: Place flour in bowl, add herbs, milk and egg, mixing until smooth. Heat a non-stick frying pan and pour in a little mixture, tilting the pan to form a pancake approximately 18 cm in diameter.

3 Cook until golden brown on both sides. Cook remaining batter to make 12 pancakes.

4 TO PREPARE FILLING: Combine cheese, zucchini and silverbeet and divide between the pancakes.

5 TO PREPARE CHILLI SAUCE: Melt butter in a saucepan and sauté garlic and onion until tender. Add flour and stir 1 to 2 minutes. Stir in remaining ingredients and heat until thickened. Keep warm

6 Fold each pancake into four and place on a baking tray. Heat in the oven for 5 to 10 minutes. Serve with sauce poured over or served separately.

SERVES 2

Savoury Pancakes

 **STORING
BUTTER**

Butter can be successfully frozen for up to 6 months, unsalted butter for 12 months. Wrap in plastic wrap or foil and date before wrapping.

Dairy Food *with* EGGS

Recipes based on eggs and dairy foods win top marks for variety, economy and flavour. Not only that, this combination is an excellent source of protein, making it a perfect substitute for meat-based meals.

Eggs have special qualities that make them invaluable ingredients. Egg whites trap and hold air most effectively, giving soufflés their light, fluffy texture; egg yolks can thicken and emulsify dressings, making them a fundamental part of many sauces. The addition of cheese, butter or cream gives texture and flavour — as rich or as piquant as you like — to these basic recipes. Milk is an important part of egg-based dishes such as omelettes and quiches, giving a rich, smooth result.

This chapter is full of delicious savoury ideas. Dairy products and eggs are ideal partners to be enjoyed at any time of day.

BÉARNAISE VARIATIONS

• *Omit tarragon added at the end of the sauce and replace it with 1 tablespoon drained, crushed green peppercorns for each cup of sauce.*

• *Add 1½ tablespoons tomato purée for each cup of sauce.*

CURDLED SAUCE

If your bearnaise, hollandaise or mayonnaise sauce curdles, correct this by whisking the sauce into another egg yolk, drop by drop. Alternatively, use a food processor.

BÉARNAISE SAUCE

Béarnaise Sauce is an excellent accompaniment to grilled or baked rich fish, such as tuna, Spanish mackerel, eel or salmon. This sauce has the same keeping qualities as Hollandaise Sauce.

WATERCRESS HOLLANDAISE

1 bunch watercress leaves

3 egg yolks

pinch salt

freshly ground black pepper

juice ½ lemon

185 g unsalted butter or cultured butter

1 Blanch watercress in boiling salted water. Drain and rinse under cold water. Squeeze out as much water as possible.

2 Place egg yolks, salt, pepper and half the lemon juice in a food processor and blend for half a minute.

3 Melt butter until foaming. With food processor motor running, add sizzling butter in a slow steady stream. Add watercress and blend until smooth. Taste sauce, adding remainder of lemon juice to taste.

5 Transfer to a bowl and serve warm. The sauce may be reheated or kept warm by placing the bowl in a small pan of simmering water.

MAKES 1 CUP (250 ML)

BÉARNAISE SAUCE

180 g butter (reduced salt butter or cultured butter can be used)

3 tablespoons vinegar

3 tablespoons dry white wine

8 black peppercorns, crushed

salt

2 tablespoons finely chopped spring onions

1½ tablespoons finely chopped fresh tarragon

3 egg yolks

1 Melt butter, remove foam from the surface and cool to tepid. Set aside.

2 Combine vinegar, wine, peppercorns, salt, spring onions and 1 tablespoon tarragon.

Boil until reduced to 2 tablespoons. Strain and cool to room temperature. Add to egg yolks and whisk for 1 minute.

3 Place mixture in the top of a double boiler. Beat vigorously over hot water until thick and creamy. The base of the pan containing mixture should never be more than hand hot.

4 Remove from heat and whisk in tepid butter, add a few drops at a time, until sauce starts to thicken, and thereafter in a very thin stream. Do not add sediment at the bottom of butter. Stir in remaining chopped tarragon.

MAKES APPROXIMATELY 1 CUP (250 ML)

MEXICAN EGGS

1 tablespoon oil

2 onions, finely chopped

1 cup (250 ml) Mexican red chilli sauce

½ cup (125 ml) tomato sauce

½ teaspoon dried oregano

310 g canned refried beans

1 tablespoon butter

60 g Cheddar cheese, grated

6 hot fried tortillas

6 eggs

1 avocado, sliced

1 Preheat oven to 180°C (350°F).

2 In a pan, heat oil and sauté onions until soft.

3 Add chilli sauce, tomato sauce and oregano. Simmer uncovered for 10 minutes, stirring occasionally.

4 Place beans in a shallow casserole dish, dot with butter and sprinkle with cheese. Bake in the oven for 10 minutes

5 Fry tortillas, place on plates, top with tomato mixture and keep warm.

6 Fry eggs, place on top of tortillas, add sliced avocado and serve with refried beans.

SERVES 6

QUICHE LORRAINE

SHORTCRUST PASTRY

1½ cups (185 g) plain flour, sifted

90 g butter, chopped

1 egg yolk

pinch salt

1 tablespoon cold water

squeeze fresh lemon juice

FILLING

250 g rindless bacon, chopped

small knob butter

2 eggs

1¼ cups (310 ml) cream

salt, pepper and nutmeg

125 g Gruyère, cheese grated

3 tablespoons chopped chives

1   TO PREPARE PASTRY: Rub butter into flour using fingertips until mixture resembles breadcrumbs. Mix remaining pastry ingredients to form a firm dough. Cover with plastic wrap and leave in refrigerator for 30 minutes.

2   Preheat oven to 200°C (400°F).

3   Roll pastry out thinly on lightly floured board and line six 8 cm individual quiche tins or one 23 cm tin. Prick with a fork and bake blind by lining with greased greaseproof paper and filling with rice or dried peas. Bake for 15 minutes. Remove rice and paper and cool.

4   TO PREPARE FILLING: Fry bacon in butter and drain on absorbent paper. Whip together eggs, cream, seasoning, cheese and chives. Arrange bacon in pastry cases and fill with cream mixture. Cook 15 minutes at 200°C (400°F) and then lower temperature to 180°C (350°F) for further 10 minutes. Serve hot or cold as an entrée or with a fresh salad as a main meal.

SERVES 6

OMELETTE AUX FINES HERBES

5 fresh eggs

¼ cup (60 ml) cream

2 tablespoons water

salt and freshly ground black pepper

30 g unsalted butter

4 tablespoons finely chopped fresh parsley, chervil, chives and tarragon

1   Break eggs into a bowl. Add cream and water, and season to taste. Beat lightly with a fork until frothy.

2   Melt butter in a 20 cm omelette pan until foaming. Pour in egg mixture, tilting pan to coat evenly. Cook until the underside is golden and the uppermost still soft.

3   Sprinkle over herbs and lightly fork through. Fold omelette in half and slide onto a warmed plate. Cut in half and serve.

SERVES 2

Omelette Aux Fines Herbes

 QUICHES

Custards or quiches should only be cooked until just set — the centre should be a little wobbly. Retained heat will complete cooking without causing overcooking.

STEP-BY-STEP TECHNIQUES

TOMATO *and* SPINACH ROULADE

6 eggs, separated

6 spring onions, finely chopped

3 spinach leaves, chopped

salt and ground black pepper

30 g Cheddar or Parmesan cheese, grated

2 cups tomato pulp or chopped tinned tomatoes

1 Preheat oven to 200°C (400°F). Line a Swiss roll tin with buttered greaseproof paper.

2 Beat egg yolks until thick. Add spring onions, spinach, seasoning and half the grated cheese. Whisk egg whites until stiff. Fold egg whites gently into egg yolk mixture. Spread mixture evenly in tin. Bake for 30 minutes.

3 Remove roulade and turn out onto a damp tea-towel. Remove paper from base. Spread tomato pulp on top. Roll up inside tea-towel. Remove tea-towel and place roulade onto a heatproof serving platter. Sprinkle over remaining cheese.

4 Return roulade to oven for 2 minutes to melt cheese. Slice roulade into portions and serve with a side salad.

SERVES 6

Place roulade on a damp tea towel.

Remove paper from base.

Roll up roulade inside tea towel.

STUFFED EGGS

5 eggs, hard-boiled, cut in half lengthways

50 g stale white bread

½ cup (125 ml) milk

1 small onion, finely chopped

50 g sausage (luncheon sausage type), finely chopped

60 g butter

500 g potatoes, boiled

2 tablespoons milk

25 g cheese, grated

1 Remove yolks and carefully remove some of the white with a teaspoon to make a hollow.

2 Rub yolks with the back of a spoon till smooth. Finely chop the removed egg white and add to yolks.

3 Soak bread in ½ cup (125 ml) milk. Fry onion and sausage in half the butter. Squeeze bread dry. Mix with onion and sausage. Add to egg mixture.

4 Mash potatoes with remaining butter and milk. Combine with cheese and egg mixture.

5 Carefully spoon mixture into egg hollows and serve.

SERVES 5

EGGS FLORENTINE

500 g spinach

30 g butter, melted

4 eggs

90 g cheese, grated

WHITE SAUCE

30 g butter, melted

1 tablespoon plain flour

½ cup (125 ml) milk

1 Preheat oven to 180°C (350°F).

2 Cook spinach until just tender, drain and purée lightly.

3 Toss in butter over low heat for a few minutes and then arrange in a shallow ovenproof dish or on four individual dishes.

4 TO PREPARE WHITE SAUCE: Melt butter in a pan. Stir in flour and cook for 1 minute. Gradually add milk, stirring constantly. Cook until thickened and smooth.

5 Make holes in the centre of spinach to form a nest and break an egg into each. Sprinkle with cheese and spoon a little sauce over each egg. Bake for 15 minutes, until eggs are set and serve immediately.

SERVES 4

CAMEMBERT OMELETTE

2 teaspoons butter

8 eggs

4 tablespoons hot water

salt and freshly ground black pepper

2 tablespoons finely chopped fresh basil

1 Camembert, cut into 4 equal portions

watercress sprigs, to garnish

1 Heat butter in a frying pan.

2 Whisk eggs with water, salt and pepper. Pour one-quarter of the mixture into foaming butter and immediately add one-quarter of the basil and one-quarter of the Camembert finely diced.

3 Lift egg mixture with a spatula once it has set to allow remaining egg to cook through. Once beginning to set, roll omelette with aid of spatula and immediately lower heat. Rolling the omelette and lowering the heat will enable the cheese to melt.

4 Place on a warm plate and serve immediately.

5 Repeat for next three omelettes. Each omelette takes 2 minutes to cook. Garnish with a sprig of watercress.

SERVES 4

DID YOU KNOW?

• *Never cook eggs in the shell in the microwave oven.*

• *Plunge hard-boiled eggs in cold water after cooking to prevent the blue-grey ring around the yolk caused by overcooking.*

• *Pastry should be rested in the refrigerator for up to 30 minutes before using to help prevent shrinkage and for butter to harden before cooking.*

• *Whole eggs need only be whisked with a fork for most uses.*

• *Store eggs in the refrigerator to keep them fresher longer.*

• *Vigorous whisking usually fixes a curdled stirred custard.*

CREAMY CURRIED EGGS

This quick and easy dish is made by combining cream cheese, cream, curry powder and pepper. Pour over sliced hard-boiled eggs and onion slices. Garnish with parsley and paprika.

CREAM CHEESE *and* SPINACH TARTS

PASTRY

1¼ cups (155 g) plain flour

¼ teaspoon salt

90 g butter, diced

2 tablespoons iced water

fresh watercress, to garnish

cherry tomatoes, to garnish

FILLING

40 g butter

3 tablespoons chopped spring onions

1½ cups spinach, cooked and drained, or
250 g frozen spinach

dash nutmeg

freshly ground black pepper

250 g cream cheese, at room temperature

4 eggs, separated

½ cup (125 ml) cream

*Cream Cheese and
Spinach Tarts*

1 TO PREPARE PASTRY: Put flour into a bowl with salt. Using your fingertips, rub butter into flour until mixture resembles coarse breadcrumbs. Add water and knead lightly. Form dough into a ball, dust with flour, wrap in greaseproof paper and chill for 1 hour.

2 Roll dough out thinly and line six small flan dishes. Prick the base of the shells and chill for 1 hour while preparing the filling.

3 Preheat oven to 200°C (400°F).

4 TO PREPARE FILLING: Melt butter in a pan over medium heat and add spring onions. When soft, add spinach, nutmeg and pepper. Cook for 5 minutes.

5 Place in a bowl and beat in cream cheese. Add egg yolks one at a time to spinach. Add cream.

6 In another bowl, beat egg whites until stiff and fold them into the spinach mixture.

7 Cover base of each flan with greaseproof paper and dried beans or rice and bake them blind for 15 minutes. Remove beans and paper and allow pastry shells to cool.

8 Fill with spinach mixture, dot with butter and bake at 180°C (350°F) for 15 to 20 minutes. Cool before serving. Garnish with watercress and cherry tomatoes.

SERVES 6

CHEDDAR SOUFFLÉ

60 g butter

¼ cup (30 g) plain flour

1 cup (250 ml) milk

125 g matured Cheddar cheese, grated

¼ teaspoon dry mustard

cayenne pepper and salt

3 eggs, separated

1 Preheat oven to 160°C (310°F).

2 Melt butter in a saucepan and blend in flour. Cook 1 to 2 minutes then add milk. Stir constantly over moderate heat till boiling.

3 Briskly beat in cheese and seasonings, to taste. Cool slightly, then beat in egg yolks.
4 Beat egg whites until firm peaks form. Fold into mixture. Pour into an 18 cm buttered soufflé dish. Bake for 50 to 60 minutes. Serve immediately with a tossed salad and hot crusty bread.

SERVES 4

PUMPKIN QUICHE SOUFFLÉ

PASTRY

1½ cups (185 g) plain flour

60 g butter

2 tablespoons lard

½ teaspoon salt

2 tablespoons cold water

FILLING

500 g butternut pumpkin, cooked until tender

20 g butter

10 spring onions, thinly sliced

salt

pinch nutmeg and ginger

3 eggs, separated

¼ cup (60 ml) cream

1 Preheat oven to 190°C (375°F).
2 Work butter and lard into flour until mixture resembles breadcrumbs. Add salt and water, form into a ball and put in refrigerator for 30 minutes. Prick base, line with foil, rice or beans, and bake blind for 15 minutes.
3 Drain pumpkin well and mash. Melt butter and cook spring onions until tender. Add to pumpkin with salt, nutmeg and ginger. Beat egg yolks and add. Beat in cream. Whisk egg whites until stiff, fold into pumpkin and pour into prepared pastry. Bake for 30 minutes until well-risen and cooked. This quiche must be served straight from the oven.

SERVES 6

Cottage Cheese Patties

COTTAGE CHEESE PATTIES

1 kg cottage cheese

5 egg yolks

2½ cups (300 g) plain flour

2 tablespoons sugar

60 g butter

¾ cup (180 ml) sour cream

1 Drain cottage cheese well, preferably overnight.
2 In a mixing bowl mix cottage cheese, egg yolks, flour and sugar. Shape into patties by rolling and shaping with the palms of the hands.
3 Fry patties in butter for about 2 minutes or until brown. Turn and fry the other side. The ideal cottage cheese patty has a fried crust and is soft in the middle. Serve hot with sour cream poured over.

SERVES 4

COTTAGE CHEESE PATTIES

These patties are a light savoury snack best served with lightly cooked vegetables or salad. The sugar can be omitted if preferred.

GELATINE

To dissolve gelatine, sprinkle it over a small amount of hot water and whisk vigorously with a fork. Both the gelatine and the mixture to be set should be at the same temperature so they blend well. Whisk vigorously to blend them. If the mixture is very cold or very hot, whisk a little of it into the gelatine solution first to equalise the temperatures.

FETTA SPINACH PIE

1 kg fresh spinach, roughly chopped

7 eggs

1 cup (250 g) fetta cheese, crumbled (reduced salt fetta can be used)

125 g Cheddar cheese, grated

oil

1 onion, chopped

freshly ground black pepper

pinch dried oregano

90 g butter

8 sheets filo pastry

1 Put spinach into a large pan. Cover and cook over low heat for 7 to 8 minutes or until spinach wilts. Drain well in a colander, pressing out the moisture with a wooden spoon.

2 In a bowl, beat eggs until fluffy. Add fetta and Cheddar.

3 Preheat oven to 190°C (375°F).

4 Heat a little oil in a pan and sauté onion until golden. Add spinach, egg-cheese mixture, pepper and oregano.

5 Melt butter and brush a baking dish with it. Lay a sheet of filo pastry on top and brush it with butter. Top with another four sheets, brushing each with melted butter and turning each sheet slightly so that the corners fan out, rather than stacking them on top of each other. Reserve three sheets.

6 Pour in spinach mixture and fold the pastry ends over it. Butter the reserved sheets of filo and place them on top to cover the dish. Slash the pastry in a few places with a sharp knife to allow the steam to escape. Brush the top with more melted butter and bake for 45 minutes. Delicious hot or cold.

SERVES 8

RAINBOW RICE PIE

½ teaspoon saffron

4 cups (1 litre) water

1 cup (185 g) brown rice

4 eggs

2 cloves garlic, crushed

4 spring onions, sliced

1 green capsicum (pepper), chopped

1 stalk celery, sliced

1 zucchini (courgette), sliced

1 carrot, grated

3 tablespoons plain flour

½ teaspoon dried oregano

1 cup (250 ml) skim milk

125 g fetta cheese, crumbled

1 Bring saffron and water to the boil. Add rice and cook for 40 minutes until tender. Drain rice and mix with one egg. Press into the base and sides of a 25 cm buttered pie plate.

2 Preheat oven to 190°C (375°F).

3 Combine garlic, spring onions, capsicum, celery and zucchini. Spoon into rice shell. Top with carrot.

4 Combine remaining ingredients and pour over vegetables. Bake for 40 to 50 minutes until set. Serve with a tossed salad and crusty bread.

SERVES 4 TO 6

BLUE CHEESE MOUSSE

2 tablespoons gelatine

1 cup (250 ml) cream

3 eggs, separated

300 g blue cheese

2 tablespoons chopped chives

¼ cup (60 ml) cream, extra

Cottage Cheese Pancakes

1 Tie a double band of greaseproof paper around each of six individual soufflé dishes to come 2.5 cm above the rim. Lightly oil inside of paper.

2 Soften gelatine in cream for 5 minutes. Stand mixture in a pan of hot water and stir until gelatine has completely dissolved.

3 Whisk egg yolks until pale, then gradually whisk in cream and gelatine mixture. Pour mixture into saucepan and stir over very low heat until thickened.

4 Mash cheese and add thickened mixture and chives. Leave to cool, then chill until beginning to set.

5 Beat egg whites until peaks form. Beat extra cream until it is just thick. Fold cream and egg whites through the cheese mixture and divide between prepared soufflé dishes. Chill until set. Before serving, remove paper.

SERVES 6

COTTAGE CHEESE PANCAKES

3 eggs, separated

125 g cottage cheese, drained

1 tablespoon plain flour

pinch cinnamon

butter

1 Blend egg yolks with cheese, flour and cinnamon.

2 Whisk egg whites until stiff peaks form and fold gently into cheese mixture.

3 Melt a little butter in frying pan. Drop batter by the large spoonful into pan and fry until golden brown on both sides, turning once. Serve immediately with honey, sour cream or yoghurt.

SERVES 4

Dairy Food with PASTA & RICE

Both pasta and rice are easy to cook; they are an important part of the diet and blend well with a wide range of ingredients to make anything from starters to desserts. For quick, tasty, nutritious meals for family and friends, pasta and rice are ideal partners with cream, milk, yoghurt and cheeses in salads, risottos, baked dishes or sauces.

This chapter offers a range of recipes, from light and simple meals to more elaborate dishes for special occasions. A sprinkling of grated fresh Parmesan cheese adds the perfect finishing touch to just about any savoury pasta or rice dish, and fresh herbs always make appetising garnishes.

CHEESE *and* PASTA TOSS

1½ cups bow noodles, cooked

1 zucchini (courgette), sliced

8 cherry tomatoes, halved

½ cup chopped fresh basil

**125 g Cheddar cheese, grated
(reduced fat cheese can be used)**

50 g canned anchovy fillets, halved

2 tablespoons prepared French dressing

1 In a salad bowl combine noodles, zucchini, tomato halves, basil and grated cheese.

2 Add anchovies. Pour over French dressing and toss gently.

SERVES 4

CHEESY RICE BALLS

2 cups (500 ml) boiling water

1 cup (185 g) short grain rice, rinsed

1 x 10 g low calorie tomato cup-a-soup sachet

40 g Parmesan cheese

130 g canned creamed corn

⅓ cup (50 g) dry breadcrumbs

1 Cook rice in boiling water with soup contents, until all water is absorbed and rice is cooked (approximately 10 to 15 minutes). Alternatively, microwave in a large bowl on HIGH (100%) for 10 to 11 minutes.

2 Remove from heat. Add cheese and corn, mixing well. Season to taste with pepper.

3 Preheat oven to 200°C (400°F).

4 Cool mixture then shape into small balls and roll in breadcrumbs. Heat in the oven for approximately 15 minutes or until heated through.

MAKES 30

 FRENCH DRESSING

Mix three parts oil with one part vinegar in a jar. Add crushed garlic, mustard, seasonings and herbs. Shake in a jar.

RICOTTA *and* VEAL PASTA PIE

1 cup (125 g) dry breadcrumbs

1 tablespoon grated Parmesan cheese

1 egg, well beaten

2 large eggplants (aubergines), cut into 3 mm slices

1 cup (250 ml) oil

250 g minced veal

1 onion, finely chopped

2 cloves garlic, crushed

125 g mushrooms, sliced

½ teaspoon dried oregano

2 tablespoons tomato paste

salt and freshly ground black pepper

250 g spaghetti

½ cup (100 g) ricotta cheese

3 eggs, hard-boiled, shelled and sliced

80 g Parmesan cheese, grated

chopped fresh parsley, to garnish

1 Combine breadcrumbs and Parmesan cheese. Lightly dip eggplant slices first into beaten egg and then into the crumb mix. Fry them in hot oil until golden brown on each side, then drain and set aside.

2 Leaving 1 tablespoon oil in the frying pan cook veal, onion, garlic, mushrooms, oregano, tomato paste, salt and pepper for 5 minutes, stirring occasionally. Reduce heat and simmer for 15 minutes.

3 Preheat oven to 190°C (375°F).

4 Boil spaghetti in salted water for 8 to 10 minutes until al dente. Drain then combine it with ricotta cheese.

5 Using a large ovenproof dish, place a layer of eggplant on the bottom, cover this with the meat mixture and top with a layer of spaghetti. Add hard-boiled eggs, sprinkle with Parmesan cheese and bake for 20 to 25 minutes, or until golden brown. Unmould onto a serving plate, cut into wedges, sprinkle with chopped parsley and serve.

SERVES 6

CREAMY CHICKEN *and* MANGO RISOTTO

60 g butter

1½ kg chicken pieces

4 tablespoons seasoned flour

1 large onion, thinly sliced

pinch nutmeg

juice and finely grated rind ½ lemon

⅔ cup (160 ml) chicken stock

salt and freshly ground black pepper

2 mangoes, sliced

⅔ cup (160 ml) cream

½ red capsicum (pepper) finely sliced, to garnish

RISOTTO

60 g butter

1 small onion, finely chopped

1½ cups (250 g) long grain rice, rinsed until water is clear

2½ cups (625 ml) chicken stock

salt and freshly ground black pepper

1 teaspoon turmeric

1 Preheat oven to 180°C (350°F).

2 Heat butter in a large, heavy-based saucepan. Toss chicken in seasoned flour until evenly coated. Gently sauté chicken pieces and onion until golden brown. Remove chicken with a slotted spoon and drain on absorbent paper, then place in a casserole dish.

3 Add nutmeg, lemon rind, stock and seasoning to pan and stir. Pour over chicken. Cover and bake for 45 minutes.

4 Add mango slices and cook a further 15 minutes. When chicken is tender, remove pieces from casserole with a slotted spoon and keep warm.

5 Return sauce to pan and bring to the boil, adding lemon juice to taste. Stir in cream and cook until sauce thickens slightly. Adjust seasonings to taste.

6 Place chicken on a serving dish and pour sauce over. Garnish with capsicum strips.

7 TO PREPARE RISOTTO: Heat butter in a saucepan and sauté onion until transparent. Add rice and stir-fry for 5 minutes over low heat. Pour in stock, stirring well and bring to the boil. Season to taste, turn heat down low, cover and simmer rice for 20 minutes or until all stock has been absorbed. Do not stir or remove lid during this time. Fluff rice gently with a fork and stir in turmeric until all the rice is coated with yellow. Serve separately with chicken.

SERVES 4

Creamy Chicken and Mango Risotto

 CHICKEN RISOTTO

This risotto is so simple. Melt some butter and brown some chicken and onion. Add red and green capsicum (pepper) and mushrooms, combine with cooked rice and season to taste.

FETTUCCINE *with* HERB SAUCE ⚖

300 g red or green fettuccine

1 tablespoon butter

2 onions, chopped

2 cloves garlic, crushed

¼ teaspoon dried thyme

¼ cup chopped fresh parsley

2½ cups (500 g) low fat cottage cheese or ricotta cheese

juice 1 lemon

salt and freshly ground black pepper

1 Cook fettuccine in boiling salted water until al dente.

2 Melt butter in a saucepan, sauté onions and garlic for 5 minutes until transparent.

3 Add thyme, parsley, cheese and lemon juice and mix well. Season to taste. Stir through hot pasta. Serve immediately with a tossed salad.

SERVES 6

PASTA *with* TOMATO *and* CREAM SAUCE

500 g pasta of your choice

SAUCE

60 g butter

2 cloves garlic, crushed

6 tomatoes, peeled and puréed

½ teaspoon salt

2 tablespoons chopped fresh basil

1 tablespoon plain flour

1 tablespoon tomato paste

1 cup (250 ml) cream (reduced fat cream can be used)

1 cup (250 ml) dry white wine

1 TO PREPARE SAUCE: Melt half the butter in a pan and sauté garlic briefly. Add tomato pulp, salt and basil. Reduce quantity to half over medium heat.

2 In a saucepan melt remaining butter and stir in flour to make a roux. Stir in tomato paste, cream, and wine. Combine with reduced tomato mixture and keep warm until ready to serve.

3 Cook pasta in boiling salted water until al dente. Drain.

4 Pour sauce over pasta and serve.

SERVES 4

SWEET *and* SOUR *with* NUTTY RICE

SWEET AND SOUR SAUCE

30 g butter

1 onion, cut into wedges

1 green capsicum (pepper), sliced

1 carrot, cut into sticks

250 g broccoli florets

230 g canned bamboo shoots

450 g canned pineapple pieces

1 tablespoon soy sauce

3 tablespoons tomato sauce

2 tablespoons white vinegar

2 tablespoons cornflour

½ cup (125 ml) water

NUTTY RICE

1 cup (185 g) rice

50 g flaked almonds, toasted

150 g Cheddar cheese, diced

1 TO PREPARE SWEET AND SOUR SAUCE: Melt butter in frying pan or wok and fry onion, green capsicum, carrot and broccoli for 3 to 4 minutes.

2 Add bamboo shoots, pineapple with juice, soy sauce, tomato sauce, vinegar and combined cornflour and water. Bring to the boil and stir until thickened.

3 TO PREPARE NUTTY RICE: Boil rice in water and toss through nuts and cheese. Serve with sauce poured over or separately.

SERVES 2 TO 4

Hot Rice Salad with Sour Cream Dressing

HOT RICE SALAD *with* SOUR CREAM DRESSING

1 cup (250 g) cooked brown rice

30 g butter

1 onion, chopped

60 g snow peas

1 small red capsicum (pepper), chopped

1 zucchini (courgette), sliced

2 spinach leaves, finely chopped

red capsicum (pepper), cut in strips, to garnish

DRESSING

2 eggs, hard-boiled and chopped

freshly ground black pepper

¼ teaspoon paprika

½ cup (125 ml) sour cream (reduced fat sour cream can be used)

1 Keep cooked rice hot in a colander over hot water.

2 Melt butter in a frying pan and add onion, snow peas, capsicum and zucchini. Cook for 5 minutes and mix with the hot rice. Add spinach to rice.

3 TO PREPARE DRESSING: Place eggs in a saucepan with pepper, paprika and sour cream. Heat but do not boil. Place salad in a serving bowl and pour over the sour cream dressing. Garnish with strips of red capsicum.

SERVES 4

SEAFOOD FETTUCCINE

♥ **SEAFOOD FETTUCCINE**

This dish may be prepared earlier in the day, covered with aluminium foil and kept in the refrigerator. Return it to room temperature before reheating.

Seafood Fettuccine

500 g thin egg noodles

125 g butter

700 g filleted white fish, cut into 2 cm pieces

white part of a small leek, sliced

⅔ cup (160 ml) dry white wine

1 cup (250 ml) fish stock

1 cup (250 ml) cream

½ teaspoon salt

pinch of cayenne

1 teaspoon fresh lemon juice

250 g prawns (shrimps) and scallops

185 g Parmesan cheese, grated

125 g butter, extra, melted

BECHAMEL SAUCE

1 tablespoon butter

1 tablespoon plain flour

1 cup (250 ml) milk

1 Cook noodles in boiling salted water for 8 minutes. Drain, rinse and cool slightly. Toss 40 g butter through and cover.

2 Heat remaining butter in pan, add fish and sauté with leek. Add wine and fish stock, bring to the boil and simmer for 1 minute. Remove fish and reduce liquid by half.

3 TO PREPARE BECHAMEL SAUCE: Melt butter in a pan. When foaming, add flour and stir over low heat for 3 minutes. Remove from heat and gradually add milk, stirring constantly. Return to heat and cook, stirring until boiling. Cook a further 3 minutes.

4 Add Bechamel Sauce to fish stock with cream, salt, cayenne and cook gently until sauce is smooth and glossy but not thick. Remove from heat, add lemon juice and strain.

5 Sauté prawns and scallops gently in butter. Do not overcook. Combine fish, prawns and scallops.

6 Preheat oven to 200°C (400°F).

7 Place one-third of the noodles in an oblong casserole, cover with half fish mixture and one-third of grated cheese, sauce and melted butter. Repeat for second layer. Top with remaining noodles, sauce and melted butter.
8 Bake for 10 to 15 minutes until golden.

SERVES 6

PASTA *with* RICOTTA SAUCE ⚖

500 g pasta of your choice
grated Parmesan cheese, to serve

SAUCE

4 tablespoons olive oil
1 small onion, chopped
500 g ricotta cheese
400 g canned tomato purée
¼ cup (60 ml) tomato paste
2½ cups (625 ml) water
salt and freshly ground black pepper

1 TO PREPARE SAUCE: Heat oil and lightly sauté onions until golden. Add ricotta, stir in tomato purée, paste and water to blend. Mix with a wooden spoon until cheese resembles coarse sand. Season to taste and cook slowly over low heat for 45 minutes.
2 Cook pasta in boiling salted water until al dente. Drain.
3 Pour sauce over pasta. Serve with Parmesan.

SERVES 4

SOYARONI CHEESE

250 g soyaroni pasta
30 g butter
2 tablespoons plain flour
1 teaspoon wholegrain mustard
3 cups (750 ml) milk
185 g Edam cheese, grated
freshly ground black pepper

1 teaspoon chopped fresh dill
1 tablespoon chopped gherkins
1 cup (60 g) soft breadcrumbs

1 Preheat oven to 180°C (350°F).
2 Cook soyaroni in boiling water until al dente. Drain and rinse.
3 Melt butter in a saucepan, stir in flour and mustard and gradually add milk. Stir constantly until sauce thickens and boils, then reduce the heat and simmer for 3 minutes. Stir in 1 cup (125 g) grated cheese, pepper, dill and gherkins.
4 Add noodles and place in four individual ramekins. Mix breadcrumbs with remaining cheese and sprinkle over the top. Bake for 15 minutes, then place under the griller to brown before serving.

SERVES 4

PUMPKIN LASAGNE ⚖

300 g pumpkin, chopped
1 large onion, chopped
250 g lasagne noodles (preferably green)
2 cloves garlic, crushed
1½ cups (300 g) fresh ricotta cheese
freshly ground black pepper
425 g canned peeled tomatoes
fresh or dried basil

1 Steam pumpkin and onion until tender. Cook noodles in boiling water until al dente.
2 Preheat oven to 180°C (350°F).
3 Purée pumpkin and onion with garlic and cheese. Season to taste with pepper.
4 Layer lasagne and pumpkin filling alternately in a lightly greased dish, finishing with lasagne.
5 Mix tomatoes with basil and cover lasagne evenly. Cover with foil.
6 Bake in oven for 30 minutes and serve hot.

SERVES 4

🍃 PASTA TIPS

• *Cook pasta in plenty of boiling, salted water. Rice can also be cooked in this manner, although the absorption method is probably the most popular.*

• *Do not break long pasta when cooking. Simply press pasta gently into boiling water.*

• *It is best to cook pasta and rice when required. If you need to keep them warm for a short period, place in a covered colander over a saucepan of simmering water.*

• *Leftover cooked pasta and rice make excellent salads. They can also be added to many cooked dishes, e.g. meatloaves, baked custard or soups.*

• *Cooked pasta tossed in butter, Parmesan and herbs makes a deliciously quick meal.*

• *When using dried herbs in place of fresh, use only a quarter of the amount.*

CANNELLONI *with* SPINACH *and* RICOTTA

SAUCE

1 small onion, finely chopped

1 clove garlic, crushed

2 tablespoons oil

500 g tomatoes, peeled and finely chopped

¼ green capsicum (pepper), finely chopped

1 bay leaf

pinch dried parsley

pinch dried oregano

pinch dried basil

⅓ cup (80 ml) water

PANCAKES

1 cup (125 g) wholemeal flour

1 egg

1 egg yolk

1 cup (250 ml) milk
(reduced fat milk can be used)

3 teaspoons butter

FILLING

500 g spinach

½ cup (100 g) ricotta or cream cheese

30 g Parmesan cheese, grated

pinch dried oregano

pinch dried basil

1 TO PREPARE SAUCE: Sauté onion and garlic in oil until soft but not brown. Add remaining ingredients, season to taste and simmer for 30 minutes.

2 TO PREPARE PANCAKES: Make a well in the flour, drop in egg and egg yolk and pour in ¼ cup (60 ml) milk. Using a fork, gradually work in the flour adding the remaining milk, a little at a time until batter is of a pouring consistency. Add more milk or water if necessary. Make eight small pancakes using more butter or oil to grease the pan in between each pancake if necessary.

3 TO PREPARE FILLING: Remove the white stalk and chop spinach leaves. Mix with the cheeses, herbs and season to taste.

4 Preheat oven to 180°C (350°F).

5 Divide filling between pancakes, roll them up and arrange in a well-buttered shallow ovenproof dish. Dot with butter and bake for 10 to 15 minutes until heated through. Spoon a little of the sauce over and serve remaining sauce separately.

SERVES 4

PUMPKIN GNOCCHI *with* RICOTTA

500 g pumpkin, to make 2 cups mashed pumpkin

1¼ cups (155 g) flour

salt

80 g Parmesan cheese, grated

½ cup (100 g) ricotta cheese

2 tablespoons chopped fresh parsley, to garnish

1 TO MAKE GNOCCHI: Peel pumpkin, and boil it in water until tender. Drain and mash pumpkin to a smooth purée with flour and salt. Knead mixture well to achieve a smooth dough. Shape dough into a log and divide it into 2.5 cm pieces.

2 Cook gnocchi in boiling salted water, a few at a time. When they rise to the surface they are ready to remove and drain.

3 Preheat oven to 200°C (400°F).

4 Place gnocchi into individual serving dishes and top each portion with Parmesan and ricotta cheeses. Bake for 10 minutes, or until golden brown. Serve sprinkled with parsley

SERVES 4 TO 6

TORTELLINI VOL-AU-VENT

Combine some butter, cream, Parmesan cheese, nutmeg, cinnamon, crushed garlic and black pepper over a low heat until smooth. Heat vol-au-vent cases. Combine sauce with cooked tortellini and spoon into cases. Sprinkle with Parmesan and return to oven for 3 minutes.

TAGLIATELLE CHEESE PUDDING

250 g white tagliatelle

125 g green tagliatelle

butter

Parmesan cheese, grated

125 g mozzarella cheese

2 tomatoes, peeled and puréed

1 tablespoon chopped fresh basil

freshly ground black pepper

125 g ricotta cheese

FRESH TOMATO SAUCE

1 large onion, grated

1 kg tomatoes, peeled and chopped

1 tablespoon finely chopped fresh basil

1 tablespoon sugar

salt

1 Cook tagliatelle separately, in boiling salted water until al dente. Drain and set aside.

2 Preheat oven to 180°C (350°F).

3 Butter a large round ovenproof dish and dust with Parmesan cheese. Cover with a layer of white tagliatelle. Top with a layer of mozzarella cheese. Cover with another layer of white tagliatelle. Pour puréed tomatoes over, sprinkle with basil and pepper. Top with a layer of green tagliatelle. Top with a layer of ricotta cheese and some more pepper. Finish off with a layer of white tagliatelle.

4 Dot generously with butter, sprinkle with Parmesan cheese, cover with foil and bake for 30 minutes. Turn out and serve with fresh tomato sauce and a salad.

5 TO PREPARE SAUCE: Purée ingredients in a food processor. Heat and serve.

SERVES 8

TROPICAL RICE SALAD ⚖

To serve this hot, toss all ingredients through hot rice or mix everything together, toss in butter and then fold yoghurt through.

½ cup (90 g) long grain brown rice, cooked

225 g canned pineapple pieces, drained

½ cup (60 g) toasted pine nuts

½ chicken, cooked and sliced

½ cup (100 g) figs

1 mango, puréed

1 cup (200 g) natural yoghurt

1 Combine all ingredients except mango and yoghurt.

2 Combine mango and yoghurt. Pour over salad and serve. This salad may also be served hot.

SERVES 4

GARLIC CREAM SAUCE

Heat oil in a pan. Sauté some garlic then stir through cream and fresh herbs (basil, marjoram, chives, chervil, coriander or thyme) and parsley. Bring to the boil, then simmer for 2 minutes. Serve over spinach tagliatelle or fettuccine.

Tropical Rice Salad

Dairy Food *with* SEAFOOD & MEATS

This chapter gives you a superb selection of dishes that can be made by combining milk, cream, butter and cheeses with all types of seafood, meat and poultry. A wide range of sophisticated results are possible using surprisingly simple techniques.

Sauté seafood, meat or poultry in butter; enrich and bind dishes with cream and yoghurt; make sauces with milk and cream; and flavour toppings, stuffings or coatings with cheese. Try using low fat sour cream or yoghurt if you are watching your fat intake. The results are just as good.

There are so many great recipe ideas here, it's hard to choose — so why not try them all!

*Unmould by running the
tip of a knife around the
edge of the moulds. Dip
moulds into warm water
for a few seconds. Shake
lightly. Invert onto
serving plate. Shake
firmly. Gently lift
off mould. If mould will
not come away, place a
hot cloth over it for
a few seconds.*

CREAMY CRAB PÂTÉ

400 g canned crab, drained

2 teaspoons fresh lemon juice

2 tablespoons chopped chives

1 cup (250 ml) mayonnaise

4 tablespoons cream

pinch curry powder

**6 teaspoons gelatine dissolved in
2 tablespoons water**

lemon rind and fresh dill sprigs, to garnish

1 In a bowl, combine crabmeat, lemon juice and chives. Fold in mayonnaise, cream, curry powder and dissolved gelatine.

3 Grease four ½ cup (125 ml) moulds lightly with oil.

4 Spoon into prepared moulds and chill. When ready, unmould and garnish with lemon and dill. Serve with toast triangles.

SERVES 4

MUSSEL SOUP *with* CRÈME FRAÎCHE

1 cup (250 ml) dry white wine

½ cup finely chopped spring onions

1½ kg mussels, cleaned, beards removed

45 g butter

2 onions, chopped

3 cloves garlic, crushed

2 leeks, well washed and chopped

2 cups (500 ml) fish stock

750 g ripe tomatoes, peeled and chopped

½ bulb fennel, chopped

2 bay leaves

1 tablespoon chopped fresh thyme

large pinch saffron threads or powder

ground black pepper

1 kg white fish fillets (whiting, snapper), cut into 2 cm pieces

**1 cup (250 ml) Crème Fraîche
(see recipe) or cream**

1 Bring wine and spring onions to the boil. Simmer 5 minutes.

2 Add mussels, cover and simmer a further 5 minutes, shaking pan occasionally to ensure even heat distribution. Discard any mussels which remain closed. Remove mussels from their shells and keep warm. Strain cooking liquid through two layers damp muslin. Reserve liquid.

3 Melt butter and sauté onions, garlic and leeks for 3 minutes. Add reserved liquid, fish stock, tomatoes, fennel, bay leaves, thyme, saffron and pepper. Simmer 30 minutes.

4 Pass the mixture through a fine sieve, pressing hard to extract as much vegetable purée as possible.

5 Reheat the mixture, add the fish pieces and simmer 5 minutes or until the fish flakes easily when tested.

6 Add the mussels and Crème Fraîche or cream. Heat through but do not boil.

SERVES 6

*Stir ¾ cup (180 ml)
cream and 1 tablespoon
natural yoghurt together
in a jar, keep covered for
8 hours in a warm place.
Or, place loosely covered
jar in a microwave and
cook on lowest setting for
4 minutes. Chill well
before using.*

CURRIED SCALLOPS

1 cup (155 g) long grain rice

1 teaspoon curry powder

2½ cups (625 ml) chicken stock

½ cup (125 ml) skim milk powder

6 spring onions, sliced diagonally

2 tablespoons chopped fresh parsley

1 cup chopped tomato

500 g scallops, cooked

2 tablespoons low fat natural yoghurt

1 Place rice, curry powder, stock and milk powder in a saucepan. Bring to the boil, cover and simmer for 15 minutes or until rice is cooked and liquid absorbed, stirring occasionally.

2 Stir remaining ingredients through rice. Heat gently and serve with a green salad.

SERVES 4

CORN *and* PRAWN CHOWDER ⚖

2½ cups (625 ml) low fat milk
(use more milk for a thinner soup)

1 large potato, diced

1 large onion, sliced

400 g canned cream corn

200 g canned or fresh prawns
(shrimps), drained

¼ cup (60 ml) fresh lemon juice

parsley or chives, to garnish

1 Place skim milk, potato, onion and corn in a saucepan and bring to the boil. Simmer for 15 minutes or until vegetables are cooked.
2 Add prawns and lemon juice, and bring to the boil. Serve garnished with parsley or chives, accompanied by wholemeal bread.

SERVES 6

SALMON *with* SORREL CREAM

4 salmon cutlets

20 g butter

1 tablespoon lime juice

SORREL SAUCE

¾ cup chopped sorrel

1 cup (250 ml) sour cream

4 strips lemon rind

cracked black pepper

1 Heat butter and juice in a frying pan until foaming. Cook salmon 2 to 3 minutes each side or until cooked.
2 Place sorrel, cream and rind in a small saucepan. Heat gently to allow sorrel to infuse for 10 to 15 minutes. Strain, season to taste with pepper and serve over salmon.

SERVES 4

Salmon with Sorrel Cream

 **WARM SALMON**

To keep the fish warm while you prepare the sauce, put it on a plate in the oven at 150°C (300°F).

SCALLOPS

You may prefer to use fresh scallops in the shell. They will be tightly closed, so you need a little help to open them. Place the shells under a pre-heated hotplate or in the oven for a few seconds. They will open so that the scallop meat can be carefully removed with a small knife. Wash them thoroughly and remove the trails leaving only the white scallop and the curved red roe. Discard the rest.

 **GRATED CHEESE**

It is best to grate cheese just before using it, however, if you are short of time, you can buy prepackaged grated cheeses, including Cheddar, Parmesan and mozzarella.

CHEESE SCALLOPS *with* CHILLI TOMATO SAUCE

CHILLI TOMATO SAUCE
1 tablespoon oil

½ onion, chopped

1 clove garlic, finely chopped

1 large tomato, peeled, seeded and chopped

pinch basil and sugar

salt and freshly ground black pepper

1 tablespoon tomato paste

1 teaspoon chilli sauce

SCALLOPS
2 egg whites at room temperature

½ cup (30 g) fresh breadcrumbs, seasoned with salt and freshly ground pepper, garlic and thyme

250 g mild cheese, grated

1 teaspoon Worchestershire sauce

18 scallops, fresh or frozen and thawed

oil for deep-frying

lemon wedges and parsley sprigs, to garnish

1 TO PREPARE SAUCE: Heat oil in a saucepan and sauté onion and garlic until onion becomes transparent.

2 Add tomato, basil, sugar, seasonings and tomato paste and cook gently for 15 to 20 minutes, adding a little water (or stock) if mixture becomes too dry. Blend in chilli sauce. If you like your sauces sharp, add an extra teaspoon of chilli sauce. Spoon mixture into an electric blender or processor and purée before serving.

3 TO PREPARE SCALLOPS: Beat egg whites until stiff. Gently fold in seasoned breadcrumbs, grated cheese and Worcestershire sauce. Mould 1 tablespoon of mixture around each scallop to form balls and deep-fry in oil heated to 165°C (325°F) for 5 minutes. Drain well on absorbent paper.

4 To serve, place three scallops on a small plate, spoon over a little Chilli Tomato Sauce and garnish with lemon wedges and sprigs of parsley.

SERVES 6

COTTAGE CHEESE *and* CRAB ROLLETTES ⚖

Use low fat mayonnaise for a healthy and low calorie dish.

250 cottage cheese (in block form, not in tub)

1 tablespoon mayonnaise

200 g canned crabmeat, drained

1 tablespoon chopped chives

225 g canned crushed pineapple

4 silverbeet or spinach leaves

½ cup (125 ml) tomato sauce

2 teaspoons chilli sauce

1 Beat cheese and mayonnaise together until smooth. Add crab meat and chives and mix thoroughly.

2 Drain pineapple reserving ¼ cup (60 ml) juice. Add pineapple to cheese mixture and stir well.

3 Cook silverbeet leaves in boiling water in a large saucepan for a couple of minutes or until tender but still bright green. Quickly rinse under cold water. Dry leaves well.

4 Spoon mixture evenly between the four leaves over the wrong side. Roll up firmly. Cut into 2 cm thick pieces.

5 Mix tomato and chilli sauces with reserved pineapple juice and serve as dipping sauce with crab rollettes.

SERVES 5

SCALLOPS *and* PRAWNS *with* TARTARE SAUCE

BATTER

2 cups (250 g) wholemeal flour, sifted

2 cups (500 ml) milk

1 egg, separated

pinch salt

pinch cayenne pepper

TARTARE SAUCE

1 cup (250 ml) mayonnaise

1 teaspoon capers, finely chopped

1 teaspoon chives

1 teaspoon French mustard

SEAFOOD

1 cup (250 ml) white wine

1 cup (250 ml) water

bouquet garni

20 scallops

20 green king prawns (large shrimps), peeled and deveined

seasoned wholemeal flour

2 cups (500 ml) oil

lemon wedges and parsley, to garnish

1 TO PREPARE BATTER: In a bowl, blend milk and egg yolk into flour and add salt and cayenne pepper. Rest for 20 minutes. Beat egg white until stiff and fold into batter.

2 TO PREPARE TARTARE SAUCE: Combine all ingredients and chill.

3 TO PREPARE SEAFOOD: In a pan, heat wine, water and bouquet garni. Poach seafood in liquid for 1 minute, remove and drain.

4 Coat seafood with seasoned flour and dip into batter. Deep-fry each piece until golden. Drain on absorbent paper.

5 Serve seafood hot with tartare sauce. Garnish with lemon wedges and parsley.

SERVES 4

Scallops and Prawns with Tartare Sauce

 DEEP-FRYING

Never fill the pan more than half to one-third full of oil.

Blanch seafood in wine mixture.

Dip seafood in flour and then batter.

Deep-fry until golden.

DID YOU KNOW?

• *Remove all fat from meat and chicken before cooking, to reduce fat and cholesterol.*

• *Raw meat slices more easily if slightly frozen.*

• *When cooking foods coated in breadcrumbs, refrigerate them for at least 15 minutes before frying or baking, to help the coating and hue.*

• *When deep-frying, test if the oil is hot enough by putting a cube of bread in it. If it sizzles, the oil is at the correct temperature.*

PECAN *and* BLUE CHEESE FILLET

2 cups (500 ml) red wine
¼ cup whole peppercorns
1½ kg eye fillet or scotch fillet
250 g blue vein cheese, crumbled
¼ cup (30 g) pecan nuts, roughly chopped

1 Combine wine and peppercorns and marinate meat for 2 hours.
2 Preheat oven to 200°C (400°F).
3 Remove meat and open out fillet lengthways. Sprinkle cheese and pecans along the centre, then close up fillet.
4 Wrap fillet in foil or secure with string. Place on a trivet in a baking dish. Bake for 40 to 50 minutes or longer if you prefer it well done.

SERVES 6 TO 8

BARBECUED PORK KEBABS

2 pork fillets, diced
1 large pear, diced
1 cup diced, cooked sweet potato
½ cup (125 ml) plum sauce
1 cup (200 g) natural yoghurt
4 tablespoons finely chopped fresh parsley
2 cups (300 g) long grain rice, cooked

1 Skewer pork, pear and potato onto eight wooden or metal sticks.
2 Heat plum sauce in a saucepan. Brush kebabs with sauce then mix remaining sauce with yoghurt.
3 Barbecue kebabs until meat is cooked through.
4 Toss parsley through cooked rice. Serve kebabs on rice and pour over sauce.

SERVES 4

LAMB *and* NUT KORMA

⅓ cup (50 g) raw, unsalted cashew nuts
3 dried chillies (hot peppers)
2 teaspoons ground coriander
1 teaspoon ground ginger
1 teaspoon cumin
½ teaspoon cinnamon
pinch ground cardamon
pinch ground cloves
2 cloves garlic, crushed
⅔ cup (160 ml) water
2 onions, chopped
60 g butter or ghee
⅔ cup (120 g) natural yoghurt
750 g lean lamb, diced
grated rind ½ lemon
2 teaspoons fresh lemon juice
½ teaspoon turmeric

1 Grind nuts and chillies together. If using a food processor add a little water.
2 Mix together coriander, ginger, cumin, cinnamon, cardamon, cloves and garlic. Add nut mixture and water and blend to a smooth paste.
3 In a pan, sauté onions in butter over low heat until they are soft but not brown. Stir in the spice and nut paste and add yoghurt. Fry over gentle heat until the oil separates.
4 Add lamb, toss well in the mixture and add lemon rind, lemon juice and turmeric. Bring to the boil, cover and simmer for 1 hour.

SERVES 4

STEP-BY-STEP TECHNIQUES

CRUMBED CHICKEN *in* BUTTER

Do not reheat this dish or keep warm for periods of time, as the butter will melt.

4 large chicken breasts

200 g butter (low salt or butter or cultured butter can be used)

1 egg yolk

½ cup (60 g) plain flour

2 eggs, beaten

dry breadcrumbs, for coating

extra butter, for frying

1 Wash and dry breasts, trim and remove skin. Place smooth side on cutting board and pound to flatten to about 5 mm thickness.

2 Combine butter with egg yolk and divide into four equal parts. Roll into sausage shapes 7 to 8 cm long. Cover each with greaseproof paper and chill until the pieces are very hard.

3 Wrap breasts around each piece of butter creating four parcels. Dip in flour, one at a time. Shake off excess flour and pat flat in the palm of the hand. Dip in beaten eggs and roll in breadcrumbs. Refrigerate for a few hours.

4 Deep-fry parcels in butter until golden brown. Serve with boiled new potatoes and steamed vegetables.

SERVES 4

Pound chicken breast to flatten.

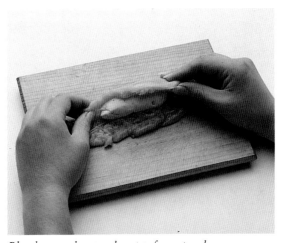

Place butter on breast and wrap to form a parcel.

Dip in flour, egg and breadcrumbs before deep-frying.

**LOW FAT
CHICKEN**

*If you are watching your
kilojoules and cholesterol,
always remove the skin
from chicken.*

CAMEMBERT CHICKEN

6 chicken fillets, skin removed

**250 g Camembert or Brie cheese,
cut into 6 sticks**

1 cup (250 ml) cranberry sauce

1 egg

2 tablespoons milk

½ cup (60 g) dry breadcrumbs

⅓ cup (30 g) desiccated coconut

1 cup (125 g) seasoned plain flour

ghee or butter for shallow frying

1 Flatten fillets between sheets of greaseproof paper until very thin. Place a Camembert stick down the centre of each and top with cranberry sauce. Roll up fillets to completely enclose filling.

2 Beat together egg and milk in a shallow dish.

3 Combine breadcrumbs and coconut in a separate dish.

4 Roll fillets into seasoned flour, dip into egg mixture then roll in crumb mixture. Dip again into egg and roll in crumbs to coat completely, pressing crumbs on firmly. Chill 30 minutes.

5 Heat ghee in a large frying pan. Cook fillets over moderately low heat until golden brown on all sides. Drain on absorbent paper. Serve immediately.

SERVES 6

Camembert Chicken

CHICKEN *and* MUSHROOMS ⚖

3 chicken fillets, skin removed

3 tablespoons seasoned plain flour

cayenne pepper

1 onion, thinly sliced

¾ cup (180 ml) tomato purée

190 g canned mushrooms, drained

1 cup (250 ml) cultured buttermilk

1 Cut chicken fillets into 1 cm strips. Place chicken pieces, flour and a pinch of cayenne pepper in a freezer bag. Toss until chicken is lightly coated in flour.

2 Cook chicken in a non-stick frypan until golden brown. Remove from pan. Add 2 tablespoons water and cook onion.

3 Blend remaining seasoned flour with a little tomato purée. Heat the rest of the tomato purée with onion, stir in flour paste, and continue stirring until thickened.

4 Return chicken to the pan. Add mushrooms and buttermilk and heat without boiling. Serve with rice or noodles and freshly steamed vegetables.

SERVES 4

SAUCY CHICKEN BALLS ⚖

250 g pasta of your choice

BALLS

400 g skinless minced chicken

200 g herb-flavoured low fat cottage cheese

1 onion, chopped

¼ cup (30 g) dry breadcrumbs

2 to 3 teaspoons Worcestershire sauce

SAUCE

440 g canned condensed soup (tomato and herb, mushroom)

1 cup (200 g) low fat natural yoghurt

1 tablespoon cornflour

1 **TO PREPARE BALLS:** Mix all ingredients together in a food processor until well blended. Shape into 40 small or 15 larger balls. Cook in a non-stick frypan until browned all over and cooked through, approximately 8 to 15 minutes. Remove from pan and set aside.

2 Cook pasta in boiling salted water until al dente, then drain.

3 **TO PREPARE SAUCE:** Add soup to the pan and stir to dissolve caramelised meat juices.

4 Blend cornflour with a little soup or water. Stir into remaining soup, simmer 3 minutes, stirring constantly. Mix in yoghurt. Heat through but do not boil.

5 Return chicken balls to pan and heat through. Serve over pasta.

SERVES 5

CREAMY TURKEY

3 tablespoons butter or margarine

1 small onion, finely chopped

500 g button mushrooms, thinly sliced

4 tablespoons plain flour

1½ cups (375 ml) turkey or chicken stock

1¾ cups (430 ml) cream

½ teaspoon salt

freshly ground black pepper

½ teaspoon chopped fresh rosemary

juice 1 lemon

3 to 4 cups cooked turkey, diced

1 Heat butter in a large pan and sauté onion gently until soft. Add mushrooms and sauté a further 2 minutes.

2 Stir in flour and cook for a few minutes. Add stock and then cream gradually, stirring constantly until sauce thickens.

3 Stir in salt, pepper, rosemary, lemon juice and turkey and simmer over low heat for 5 minutes. Serve with fluffy rice.

SERVES 6

 GHEE

Ghee is clarified butter. If you want to clarify your own, heat butter until melted and frothy. Set aside until cool. Scoop sediment from top and discard. Use remainder as directed.

 SAUCY CHICKEN BALLS

Cottage cheese can be bought with various herb flavours already added, or you can buy plain low fat cottage cheese and add fresh chopped herbs such as parsley or mint.

*Green peppercorns are
usually only available in
cans and have a mild,
aromatic flavour.
Steaks thicker than 1 cm
should be fried for twice
given length of time, or
beaten with a rolling pin
or meat mallet to given
thickness. For a medium-
cooked steak, fry for
4 minutes. For a well-
cooked steak, cover the
pan while frying for 4 to
5 minutes.*

*Steak with Green
Pepper Sauce*

STEAK *with* GREEN PEPPER SAUCE

**4 sirloin steaks, 1 cm thick, trimmed of fat
and sinew**

¼ cup (60 ml) oil

pinch salt

50 g butter

3 tablespoons brandy

**½ cup (125 ml) dry sherry or dry
Madeira wine**

1 tablespoon chopped parsley, to garnish

SAUCE

1 onion, chopped

2 tablespoons green peppercorns, canned

2 tablespoons soy sauce

1 teaspoon vinegar

⅔ cup (160 ml) cream

pinch paprika

1 Brush steaks with a little oil and season
very lightly with salt.
2 Heat remaining oil and butter in a frying
pan and quickly fry steaks on both sides for
about 2 minutes. Pour in brandy and set it

alight. Almost immediately pour in sherry
to put out brandy flames. Remove steaks and
keep them warm while cooking sauce.
3 TO PREPARE SAUCE: Add onion,
peppercorns, soy sauce and vinegar to pan
mixture. Boil for 4 minutes. Add cream and
paprika and boil briskly for another minute.
4 Return steaks to sauce to reheat for a
minute on each side. Serve immediately,
garnished with parsley.

SERVES 4

VEAL *with* APPLE *and* CALVADOS

*Apple cider can be substituted for apple brandy but
it will not ignite.*

6 veal escalopes

125 g butter

salt and pepper

**2 to 3 tablespoons calvados (apple brandy)
or apple cider**

½ cup (125 ml) cream

1 apple, peeled, cored and sliced into rings

1 Pat veal dry with absorbent paper.
2 Melt half the butter over high heat. Add
veal and quickly sauté until golden on both
sides. Season with salt and pepper.
3 Add brandy, ignite and flame. When the
flames die away, add cream and swill pan
from side to side. Reduce heat to low and
simmer for 2 to 3 minutes. If you prefer a
thicker sauce, remove veal from pan and boil
sauce until reduced.
4 Melt remaining butter in a separate pan.
Add apples and cook over high heat for
3 minutes or until golden. Spoon apples
onto a heated serving dish. Place veal on top
and serve with sauce spooned over.

SERVES 6

Barbecued Beef with Horseradish Cream Sauce

BARBECUED BEEF *with* HORSERADISH CREAM SAUCE

1½ kg beef fillet or thick piece rump steak

4 to 6 rashers bacon

MARINADE

1 carrot, roughly chopped

1 onion, roughly chopped

1 cup (250 ml) port

½ cup (125 ml) oil

few peppercorns

1 teaspoon whole allspice

1 clove garlic, crushed

HORSERADISH CREAM SAUCE

1 cup (250 ml) thickened cream, whipped and chilled

1 tablespoon grated horseradish root

1 spring onion, finely chopped

1 tablespoon finely chopped fresh parsley

1 Trim beef of excess fat and all sinew.

2 Place beef on a board and wrap bacon around in a spiral. Secure with toothpicks.

3 Combine all marinade ingredients and place with beef in a shallow ceramic bowl. Cover with plastic wrap and marinate in the refrigerator overnight, turning beef from time to time. Remove beef from marinade and pat dry with absorbent paper.

4 Cook beef over moderately hot barbecue coals for about 10 to 12 minutes for a medium rare steak or 15 to 20 minutes for a medium steak. Test with a skewer then remove from barbecue and stand meat for 10 minutes before carving.

5 Carve thin slices across the grain. Arrange on a platter and serve with Horseradish Cream Sauce.

6 TO PREPARE SAUCE: Combine all ingredients, stir until blended and serve in a bowl.

SERVES 10

HORSERADISH SOUR CREAM DRESSING

Beat 1¼ cups (300 ml) sour cream with 3 tablespoons grated horseradish and a squeeze of lemon juice. Season with salt and freshly ground pepper. Serve with beetroot and other salads.

SWEET DAIRY TASTES

Name your favourite dessert, and it is sure to feature the unmistakable flavour and texture of dairy food: fluffy soufflés and delicious fruit flans, tempting ice creams and light, lacy crêpes — they all depend on milk, cheese and cream.

In this chapter you will discover how to make your own ice cream in a few simple steps using a stirred milk/egg custard as the base. You can also make very quick ice creams by blending whipped cream with fruit or flavourings of your choice. By making these desserts yourself, you know that everything is fresh and free from artificial additives.

These wonderful sweet treats can be served all year round. Where fruit is called for, choose fruit in season for the freshest, tastiest result. Whatever 'sweet taste' you choose, you are sure to delight family and friends — and they'll be sure to ask for more.

GINGER SOUFFLÉ

60 g butter

3 tablespoons plain flour

1½ cups (375 ml) milk

2 tablespoons sugar

3 eggs, separated

1 teaspoon vanilla essence

2 teaspoons grated ginger in syrup

icing sugar, sifted

1 Preheat oven to 190°C (375°F).

2 Melt butter in a saucepan, stir in flour and cook for 1 minute. Add milk gradually, stirring constantly, to form a smooth sauce. Add sugar and stir until it dissolves. Cool the sauce slightly.

3 Beat egg yolks into the sauce with vanilla essence and ginger.

4 Beat egg whites until stiff and fold them into the sauce.

5 Spoon mixture into a soufflé dish and bake for 40 minutes. Sprinkle with icing sugar and serve immediately.

SERVES 4 TO 6

MINI CHOCOLATE POTS

125 g dark or cooking chocolate

2½ cups (625 ml) milk

2 eggs

2 egg yolks

2 tablespoons caster sugar

2 teaspoons rum

½ cup (125 ml) cream, whipped, to garnish

1 Preheat oven to 160°C (325°F).

2 Grate one square of chocolate for decoration. Place milk and remaining chocolate in the top of a double boiler. Heat gently, stirring, until chocolate melts.

3 Beat eggs, egg yolks and sugar together until light, then pour in hot but not boiling milk, stirring all the time. Stir in rum, then strain mixture into six individual ovenproof dishes.

4 Stand dishes in a roasting pan half-filled with hot water, bake for 40 to 60 minutes or until custards are lightly set.

5 Serve hot or cold, decorate with whipped cream and grated chocolate.

SERVES 6

MERINGUES *in* CUSTARD

5 eggs, separated

⅔ cup (155 g) caster sugar

3 cups (750 ml) milk

few drops vanilla essence

1 Place yolks and half the sugar in a bowl and whisk until they are creamy. Whisk egg whites in another bowl until they are stiff, add remaining sugar and continue to whisk until meringue is very stiff.

2 Bring milk and vanilla to the boil, reduce heat and drop 4 tablespoonfuls of meringue mixture into saucepan. Let meringues poach for 5 minutes on either side. Remove them with a draining spoon and place them on a clean cloth to dry.

3 Return milk to boil and gradually whisk it into egg yolk mixture. Return this mixture to saucepan and cook it over a low heat, stirring constantly with a wooden spoon until custard is smooth and coats spoon.

4 Strain custard and pour it into four individual serving dishes. Allow custard to cool. Place a poached meringue on top of each dish and chill in refrigerator for 1 hour before serving.

SERVES 4

CRÈME CARAMEL

½ cup (125 ml) water

2¾ cups (685 g) sugar

4 eggs

1 egg yolk

3 tablespoons water

vanilla essence

2¼ cups (680 ml) milk

1¼ cups (300 ml) cream, whipped
for serving

SPUN SUGAR

1 cup (220 g) caster sugar

pinch cream of tartar

½ cup (125 ml) water

1 Bring water and 1 cup (250 g) sugar to the boil in a heavy-based saucepan. Boil without stirring until mixture is a rich golden caramel colour. Pour caramel into one large mould, coating the base and sides, or into eight individual ramekin dishes. Set aside to cool.

2 Preheat oven to 180°C (350°F).

3 Combine eggs and egg yolk, remaining sugar, 3 tablespoons water and vanilla essence. Heat milk, without boiling, and gradually whisk into egg mixture. Strain and pour into mould.

4 Place mould in a baking tin half-filled with water and bake 40 to 50 minutes, or until set. Individual moulds will only take 20 minutes to cook. Test by inserting a butter knife into the custard. If the knife comes out clean, the custard is set.

5 Chill thoroughly before turning out onto serving dish. Pour any caramel remaining in the mould around the dish and decorate with Spun Sugar if desired. Serve with whipped cream.

6 TO PREPARE SPUN SUGAR: Combine all ingredients in a small saucepan and heat, gently stirring until the sugar dissolves. Using a wet pastry brush, brush away any

remaining crystals from the side of the pan as these will cause the syrup to crystallise. Increase the heat and boil until a rich golden colour. Cool slightly. Working over sheets of baking paper dip two forks into the syrup, join together then draw apart to form fine threads of toffee. Work quickly before the toffee sets and remember that it is very hot. When all the toffee has been used carefully lift the threads from the paper and place a little on top of each crème caramel.

NOTE: Do not attempt this if the weather is humid as the spun sugar will dissolve within moments of making. Prepare just before serving.

SERVES 8

Crème Caramel

 BAKED CUSTARDS

Baked custards such as crème caramel, should be baked in a water bath as direct heat will cause the dish to cook too fast and curdle. Place the crème caramel dishes in a baking dish with enough warm water to come half way up the sides of the containers. When cooked, remove from water to prevent overcooking from retained heat.

CHOCOLATE CARAQUÉ

Grate 60 g cooking chocolate into a warmed plate placed over a saucepan of hot water. When melted, spread on marble or on a metal baking tray which has been refrigerated. When chocolate has set, scrape off into pieces with a sharp knife or a melon baller.

CHOCOLATE TORTE

5 eggs, separated

1 cup (220 g) sugar

250 g dark cooking chocolate, melted

½ teaspoon vanilla essence

½ cup (60 g) plain flour, sifted

1 teaspoon bicarbonate of soda

½ teaspoon cream of tartar

CREAM

½ cup (100 g) sugar

⅓ cup (80 ml) milk

200 g butter

1 tablespoon cocoa powder

½ teaspoon cognac

CHOCOLATE GLAZE

1 cup (220 g) sugar

60 to 80 g unsalted butter

2 tablespoons cocoa powder

1 tablespoon milk

DECORATION

whipped cream

½ cup (70 g) toasted almonds, finely chopped

1 Preheat oven to 180°C (350°F).

2 Beat egg yolks vigorously with ⅔ cup (160 g) sugar until creamy, add two-thirds of the melted chocolate and vanilla and mix well.

3 In another mixing bowl, whip egg whites until stiff with remaining sugar and add to

Chocolate Torte

chocolate mixture. Fold in flour, bicarbonate of soda, cream of tartar and remaining chocolate.

4 Line a Swiss roll pan (24 cm x 30 cm) with greaseproof paper and pour the mixture into it. Bake for 30 to 40 minutes.

5 TO PREPARE CREAM: Mix sugar and milk until sugar dissolves. Add butter, cocoa and cognac and beat well until mixture is smooth.

6 When cake is cool, cut in half and spread with prepared cream, using a wet knife to spread. Then stack one piece on top of the other.

7 TO PREPARE CHOCOLATE GLAZE: Beat sugar with butter until sugar dissolves. Mix cocoa and milk together in a cup and add to the butter mixture. Beat until smooth then spread on cake using a spatula. Cover the whole torte with whipped cream and sprinkle with almonds or chocolate caraqué.

SERVES 6 TO 8

YOGHURT HONEY ICE

⅔ cup (160 ml) honey
6 egg yolks
3 cups (600 g) natural yoghurt

1 Heat honey in a pan on low heat to almost boiling.

2 Whisk egg yolks until pale and frothy. Beat in the honey gradually and continue beating until cool.

3 Whisk in yoghurt and place mixture in freezer. Take it out regularly during the freezing process and beat with a fork to prevent ice crystals forming. Alternatively, use an ice cream maker, following the manufacturer's instructions.

MAKES 4 CUPS (1 LITRE)

BAKED LEMON CHEESECAKE

BASE
150 g butter, melted
200 g Marie or plain sweet biscuits, crushed

FILLING
250 g cream cheese, softened at room temperature
250 g cottage cheese
3 eggs, lightly beaten
¾ cup (185 g) sugar
1 tablespoon cornflour
½ cup (125 ml) sour cream
grated rind 1 lemon
3 tablespoons fresh lemon juice
3 tablespoons lemon butter

1 TO PREPARE BASE: Combine melted butter with biscuit crumbs. Press into the base and sides of a 21 cm x 5 cm round ovenproof dish (or 23 cm springform tin). Refrigerate.

2 Preheat oven to 180°C (350°F).

3 TO PREPARE FILLING: Beat cream cheese until smooth. Blend in cottage cheese, eggs, sugar, cornflour, sour cream, lemon rind and 1 tablespoon lemon juice. Beat until smooth.

4 Pour onto biscuit base. Bake for 55 to 60 minutes or until set. Cool before removing cheese cake from dish.

5 Blend remaining lemon juice with lemon butter in a small saucepan. Heat gently, stirring until melted and combined. Pour over top of cheese cake. Chill thoroughly before serving.

SERVES 8

 YOGHURT ICE CREAMS

Yoghurt is one of nature's gifts. A good source of protein, it also contains bacteria which are beneficial to our digestive system. Besides its many other uses, yoghurt forms the basis of a delightful alternative to ice cream, when used in yoghurt ice. Low fat yoghurt can also be used, but should be mixed with whisked egg white to soften the texture.

Tropical Yoghurt Flan

TROPICAL YOGHURT FLAN

CRUST

100 g butter, melted

250 g packet chocolate biscuits, crushed

1 egg yolk

FILLING

2 tablespoons custard powder

2 tablespoons caster sugar

1 cup (250 ml) milk

3 teaspoons gelatine

2 tablespoons hot water

½ cup (125 ml) pineapple juice

1 cup (250 ml) tropical yoghurt

shredded coconut, to decorate

1 Preheat oven to 180°C (350°F).

2 TO PREPARE CRUST: Mix butter with biscuit crumbs and egg yolk and press into base and sides of a buttered 25 cm pie dish. Bake for 10 minutes. Cool.

3 TO PREPARE FILLING: Blend custard powder, sugar and milk in a small saucepan until smooth. Cook over medium heat, stirring constantly, until boiling. Simmer for 3 minutes.

4 Whisk gelatine into water. Beat into custard with pineapple juice. Cool slightly.

5 Blend in yoghurt. Pour into pie crust. Chill until set. Top with shredded coconut.

SERVES 8

CREAMY FRUIT BRULÉ

Use any fruit in season for this dessert: grapes, peeled and seeded; cherries, seeded; apricots, quartered; strawberries, hulled; kiwi fruit, peeled and sliced.

4 cups prepared fruit

1 cup (250 ml) cream

4 tablespoons brown sugar

¼ teaspoon cinnamon

SPUN TOFFEE

½ cup (125 g) sugar

water

1 Place fruit into four individual ovenproof serving dishes and pour ¼ cup (60 ml) cream into each. Chill overnight.

2 Just before serving, sprinkle 1 tablespoon brown sugar and a little cinnamon over each and place under the griller until the sugar melts and browns. Garnish with spun toffee.

3 TO PREPARE SPUN TOFFEE: Heat sugar in a saucepan. Brush edges with water using a pastry brush to dissolve crystals. Stir until sugar is dissolved. When toffee is boiling do not stir. Heat gently until a golden brown. It should be tacky when two spoons are touched together. Remove from the heat and spin toffee using spoons. Cut strands with scissors and arrange on top of fruit.

SERVES 4

Creamy Fruit Brulé

FRUIT COULIS

Make a quick fruit coulis to serve with all kinds of dessert, including ice cream, by processing fruit or berries of your choice with a little brandy, sherry or fruit juice. If it needs sweetening, whisk in a little icing sugar.

PROFITEROLES *and* CHOCOLATE RUM SAUCE

CHOUX PASTRY

⅔ cup (80 g) plain flour

⅔ cup (160 ml) water

75 g butter, unsalted

3 to 4 eggs, slightly beaten

FILLING

1¼ cups (310 ml) cream, whipped

1 tablespoon caster sugar

SAUCE

250 g plain chocolate, chopped

3 tablespoons rum

1 tablespoon caster sugar

25 g butter, unsalted

1 TO PREPARE PASTRY: Sift flour onto a piece of greaseproof paper. In a saucepan heat water, salt and butter until butter melts. Remove pan from heat and add all flour at once. Beat vigorously with a wooden spoon until mixture is smooth. Return pan to low heat and beat until mixture pulls away from sides of pan to form a ball. Cool to tepid.

2 Beat in eggs, a little at a time, beating well between each addition. The mixture should be glossy and hold its shape when dropped from the spoon. Use as required.

NOTE: All the egg may not be needed. The mixture will not hold its shape if too much egg is added.

3 Preheat oven to 200°C (400°F).

4 On a greased baking sheet, put 18 heaped teaspoons of Choux Pastry, well separated.

5 Bake for 20 minutes until well risen and golden brown. Remove from oven, make a small slit in each to allow steam to escape. Return to oven for 5 minutes to dry out, then cool.

6 Just before serving, whip the cream with sugar until stiff. Using a piping bag, fill each profiterole through side slit and pile them on a dish.

7 TO PREPARE SAUCE: Melt chocolate and rum in a bowl over a saucepan of boiling water. Add sugar and butter and mix well. Pour over profiteroles and serve cold.

MAKES 18

APPLE YOGHURT ICE ⚖

700 g green cooking apples, cored and sliced

¼ teaspoon nutmeg

¼ teaspoon cinnamon

⅔ cup (150 g) sugar

grated rind 1 orange

juice 2 oranges

2 cups (400 g) natural yoghurt

1 Place apples in saucepan with spices and sugar. Add orange rind and orange juice to the apple. Bring to the boil gradually and simmer until soft. Cool, blend and sieve.

2 Add yoghurt and pour mixture into a chilled container. Place in freezer. Take it out at regular intervals and beat with a fork to prevent formation of crystals. Alternatively, use an ice cream maker, following the manufacturer's instructions.

MAKES 4 CUPS (1 LITRE)

BASIC VANILLA ICE CREAM

2 cups (500 ml) milk

1 vanilla bean split lengthways or 1½ to 2 tablespoons vanilla essence

1 cup (200 g) caster sugar

6 egg yolks

1 cup (250 ml) cream

1 Heat milk in a saucepan with vanilla bean and half the sugar. Bring to the boil, cover the pan, turn off heat and rest 15 minutes.

2 Beat egg yolks and remaining sugar in a bowl until thick and light.

3 Bring milk back to the boil and whisk a small amount into egg and sugar mixture. Remove the saucepan of milk from the heat and whisk the egg-sugar mix into it.

4 Return the saucepan to a low heat, stirring constantly; do not allow to boil. As the custard cooks it will thicken slowly. It should coat the back of a spoon when cooked. Remove the pan from the heat and place in a bowl of cold water. Take out vanilla bean.

5 To prepare by hand, whip cream until firm, then fold into cooled custard, chill and freeze. If using an ice cream maker, pour cream into custard, chill and freeze, following the manufacturer's instructions.

MAKES 4 CUPS (1 LITRE)

CUSTARD-BASED ICE CREAMS

To make these ice creams, it is important to cook the custard accurately. Either use a sugar thermometer (temperature should not exceed 85°C (170°F)) or test it by dipping a wooden spoon in the custard, then let it run off and draw a line on the spoon with your finger. If the line holds, the custard is cooked.

If the custard curdles from overheating, remove from heat, take out the vanilla bean, add a tablespoon of cold milk and blend until smooth.

Whisk a small amount of milk into egg and sugar mixture.

Test custard for consistency — it should coat the back of the spoon.

MAKING ICE CREAM

Although the quickest way of making ice cream is in an ice cream machine, it is not essential. If you don't have one, place the mixture in the freezer for 2 to 3 hours, then take out and beat well with a fork, return to freezer and repeat this until the ice cream is of the consistency you like. This method is called 'still-freezing'.

CONTINENTAL CHOCOLATE ICE CREAM

2½ cups (625 ml) milk

1 cup (200 g) sugar

6 egg yolks

175 g dark cooking chocolate, chopped

1 cup (250 ml) cream

1 Heat milk in a pan. Beat egg yolks with sugar in a bowl. Add egg-sugar mixture to the milk and cook until it thickens slightly.

2 Melt chocolate in the top half of a double boiler. Place half the hot custard in a bowl and whisk in chocolate quickly. Return chocolate custard to the custard on the stove and stir gently to incorporate.

3 Remove from heat, cool and add cream.

4 Still-freeze or use an ice cream maker, following the manufacturer's instructions.

MAKES 4 CUPS (1 LITRE)

COFFEE ICE CREAM

4 egg yolks

⅓ cup (90 g) caster sugar

½ cup (125 ml) milk

½ cup (125 ml) cream

3 tablespoons instant coffee powder

1 teaspoon vanilla essence

2 cups (500 ml) cream

1 Place egg yolks, sugar, milk, cream and coffee powder in a bowl over hot water.

2 Beat with a whisk for 10 minutes until thickened and doubled in volume.

3 Chill mixture and add cream.

4 Still-freeze or use an ice cream maker, following the manufacturer's instructions.

MAKES 4 CUPS (1 LITRE)

BANANA ICE CREAM

2 cups (500 ml) milk

⅔ cup (150 g) sugar

4 egg yolks

650 g bananas

1 ½ tablespoons fresh lemon juice

1 Heat milk in a pan. Beat egg yolks and sugar in a bowl and add to milk. Heat until mixture thickens, then cool.

2 When it is cold, peel bananas and quickly purée with lemon juice in a food processor.

3 Place banana purée in a bowl and gradually add custard, whisking constantly to obtain a smooth texture.

4 Still-freeze or use an ice cream maker , following the manufacturer's instructions.

MAKES 4 CUPS (1 LITRE)

LEMON YOGHURT GELATI

½ cup (125 ml) water

finely grated rind ½ lemon

¼ cup (60 ml) fresh lemon juice

2 teaspoons gelatine

1 cup (200 g) low fat apricot yoghurt

liquid sweetener or 2 tablespoons of sugar

2 egg whites

1 Combine water, lemon rind and juice in a small saucepan. Sprinkle gelatine on top. Heat gently, stirring until gelatine dissolves. Cool slightly.

2 Stir in yoghurt till smooth. Blend in liquid sweetener.

3 Pour into a wide-based stainless steel or plastic container. Freeze until ice crystals form in 1 cm thick layer around the sides.

4 Remove from freezer and beat thoroughly with a hand or electric beater for 1 to 2 minutes.

Rich Honey Ice Cream

5 Whisk egg whites till stiff peaks form. Gently fold into mixture. Freeze for several hours till firm. Serve in an ice cream cone or in chilled dessert glasses.

SERVES 4 TO 6

RICH HONEY ICE CREAM

½ cup (125 ml) milk

¾ cup (180 ml) honey

6 egg yolks

fresh lemon juice, to taste

2½ cups (625 ml) cream

1 Place milk and honey in a saucepan and bring slowly to the boil, stirring constantly.

2 Whisk egg yolks in a bowl until thick and light. Whisk in honey-milk mixture. Return mixture to a rinsed pan over a low heat, whisking until thickened.

3 Remove and chill. Add lemon juice and cream, and mix well.

4 Place mixture a tray and freeze, taking it out regularly to beat with a fork. Alternatively, use an ice cream maker, following the manufacturer's instructions.

MAKES 4 CUPS (1 LITRE)

CHOCOLATE GELATO

♥ **CHOCOLATE GELATO**

A low calorie version of this can be made by substituting skim milk for full cream milk.

3 cups (750 ml) milk

1 cup (250 g) sugar

125 g unsweetened cooking chocolate, chopped

1 Heat milk and sugar gently in a saucepan until sugar dissolves.

2 In the top half of a double boiler melt chocolate slowly on low heat, until smooth.

3 Gradually add sweetened milk to chocolate, stirring constantly. Cook over medium heat until well combined.

4 Chill in refrigerator and then still-freeze (take out of freezer and beat regularly with a fork) or use an ice cream maker and freeze, following the manufacturer's instructions.

MAKES 4 CUPS (1 LITRE)

Chocolate Gelato and Strawberry Gelato

STRAWBERRY GELATO

2 cups (500 ml) milk

¾ cup (175 g) sugar

1½ cups (125 g) skim milk powder

500 g strawberries, hulled and puréed

1 tablespoon fresh lemon juice

1½ teaspoons vanilla essence

1 Gently heat milk, sugar and skim milk powder until dissolved. Chill 30 minutes.

2 Stir in strawberries, lemon juice and vanilla.

3 Mix thoroughly, still-freeze (take out of freezer and beat regularly with a fork) or place in an ice cream maker and freeze, following the manufacturer's instructions.

MAKES 4 CUPS (1 LITRE)

LOW FAT FROZEN BANANA YOGHURT ⚖

2 cups (400 g) low fat vanilla yoghurt

3 bananas, mashed

¼ cup (60 g) sugar

375 g canned evaporated reduced fat milk, well chilled

1 Mix yoghurt, bananas and sugar together well.

2 Whip evaporated milk until thick and creamy. Fold in yoghurt mixture, pour into ice cream trays and freeze for 2 hours.

3 Whip again until frothy. Freeze until solid. Serve with fresh fruit and almond bread or thin wafers if desired.

SERVES 10

CHOCOLATE SAUCE

1½ tablespoons caster sugar

1½ cups (375 ml) milk

½ cup (125 ml) cream

40 g unsalted butter, melted

200 g cooking chocolate, chopped

1 Place sugar, milk, cream and butter in a saucepan, stir to dissolve. Bring to the boil.

2 Reduce heat, add chocolate and stir until it melts. Cool sauce and serve cold.

MAKES 3 CUPS (750 ML)

BUTTERSCOTCH SAUCE

1½ cups (250 g) brown sugar

½ cup (125 ml) glucose or corn syrup

60 g unsalted butter

pinch salt

¼ cup (60 ml) water

2 teaspoons vanilla essence

½ cup (125 ml) cream

1 Mix sugar, glucose, butter, salt and water in a saucepan and bring to the boil.

2 Remove from heat and stir in vanilla and cream. Serve warm or cold.

MAKES 1½ CUPS (375 ML)

WARM FUDGE SAUCE

½ cup (125 ml) cream

45 g unsalted butter

⅓ cup (90 g) sugar

½ cup (90 g) brown sugar

pinch salt

½ cup (60 g) cocoa powder

1 Heat cream and butter in a saucepan over medium heat until boiling.

2 Add white and brown sugar, gently heating to dissolve. Whisk in salt and cocoa to dissolve. Serve warm.

MAKES 1½ CUPS (375 ML)

COLD COFFEE SAUCE

1 cup (200 g) sugar

1 cup (250 ml) water

2 tablespoons coffee powder

30 g unsalted butter

½ cup (125 ml) cream

1 Combine sugar and water in a saucepan over medium heat. Stir constantly, cooking for 5 minutes.

2 Add coffee, stir to dissolve, remove from heat. Gradually stir in butter then cream.

3 Store in refrigerator until required.

MAKES 1½ CUPS (375 ML)

❤ ICE CREAM TIPS

• *Chill all ice cream making equipment — bowls, whisk, spatulas.*

• *Cool custard base by plunging bowl into a basin of cold water.*

• *Turn freezer setting to its coldest setting or quick freeze position.*

• *Metal containers will freeze ice creams quicker but don't use metal if there is acidic fruit in the mixture.*

• *Homemade ice cream should be made and frozen at least a day before eating to allow the ice cream to set and ripen.*

• *Ice cream should always be removed from the freezer and kept in the refrigerator for 30 minutes to allow slow softening before serving.*

A BAKER'S DOZEN

Dairy foods and baking go hand in hand. Nothing creams better than butter — it holds air and adds a feel and flavour that no substitute can. Milk is an important liquid in many recipes. Quite often, sour cream, yoghurt or buttermilk can be substituted for a denser, richer result. And of course, low fat products can be substituted in most recipes.

It is a hospitable tradition to have cakes, cookies and a fresh batch of scones ready for every visitor. Why not take time to enjoy the rewarding feeling of baking home-made goodies and enticing the family with the homely aroma of baking? You will find that 'homemade' tastes better and is healthier than 'ready-made', and that successful baking depends on fresh dairy products.

Happy baking!

Store these crisp biscuits in an airtight tin, after cooling.
When rubbing butter into flour, always use finger-tips only, to prevent the butter from melting before the flour particles are coated. Use a light hand when mixing for the best results.

CARAWAY CHEESE BISCUITS

¾ cup (90 g) plain flour
¼ cup (30 g) self-raising flour
¼ cup (30 g) cornflour
pinch salt
pinch cayenne or chilli powder
125 g butter
1 teaspoon caraway seeds
125 g Cheddar cheese, grated
30 g Parmesan cheese, grated
extra caraway or sesame seeds, to sprinkle

1 Preheat oven to 180°C (350°F).
2 Sift flours together with salt and cayenne into a bowl. Rub in butter until mixture resembles fine breadcrumbs. Add caraway seeds. Stir cheeses into the mixture using a knife until mixture gathers into a ball.
3 Pinch off walnut-sized pieces of dough and roll into balls. Place on greased baking trays and press out lightly using the back of a fork. Sprinkle with extra caraway seeds and bake for 12 to 15 minutes, or until golden brown. Cool on a wire rack and store in an airtight tin.

MAKES 30

CARAWAY SOUR MILK CAKE

2 cups (250 g) plain flour

2 teaspoons nutmeg

1 teaspoon bicarbonate of soda

1 teaspoon baking powder

125 g butter (low salt butter or cultured butter can be used)

1 teaspoon vanilla essence

1 cup (220 g) caster sugar

½ cup (85 g) brown sugar

3 eggs

1 teaspoon caraway seeds

½ cup (125 ml) milk, soured with 1 teaspoon lemon juice

TOPPING

⅓ cup (90 g) sugar

1½ teaspoons cinnamon

2 teaspoons grated orange rind

¾ cup (45 g) soft breadcrumbs

40 g butter (low salt or cultured butter can be used), melted

1 Preheat oven to 200°C (400°F). Grease and line a 20 cm cake tin.

2 Sift flour, nutmeg, bicarbonate and baking powder twice into a bowl.

3 In another bowl, cream butter, vanilla and sugars until light and fluffy. Beat in eggs.

4 Fold in flour mixture and caraway seeds alternately with sour milk. Place mixture in prepared cake tin.

5 Bake for 35 to 40 minutes. Halfway through cooking time, sprinkle over combined topping ingredients and return to oven. Test with a skewer to see if cooked. Cool on a cake rack and serve.

SERVES 6 TO 8

Caraway Cheese Biscuits
and Caraway Sour Milk Cake

CASHEW-NUT FUDGE

2 cups (500 g) sugar

4 tablespoons water

4 tablespoons rose water

2 cups (250 g) raw cashew nuts, ground

250 g butter

2 tablespoons shelled walnuts

½ teaspoon salt

1 tablespoon hot milk

1 TO PREPARE SYRUP: Gently heat sugar and water in a medium-sized saucepan, stirring, until mixture comes to the boil. Simmer, without stirring, for 3 minutes.

2 Add rose water to ground cashews and mix well. Add cashew mixture to syrup and cook, stirring constantly, till thickened. Add butter gradually, a little at a time. Stir in the walnuts, salt and milk and remove from the heat after 1 minute.

3 Pour into greased 20 cm square dish and refrigerate. Score into diamond shapes before fudge hardens. Serve cold, cut in diamonds.

MAKES ABOUT 24

GOLDEN OAT SLICE

180 g butter

1 tablespoon golden syrup

½ cup (90 g) brown sugar

1 cup (90 g) rolled oats

pinch mixed spice

1 Preheat oven to 190°C (375°F).

2 Melt butter, golden syrup and brown sugar in a saucepan.

3 Add rolled oats and mixed spice and combine.

4 Pour into greased baking tray and bake for 20 minutes, until golden brown. Cut into 10 fingers while still warm.

MAKES 10

BAKING TIPS

• *Cool baked goodies well on a wire rack. Store in an airtight container.*

• *Most baked goodies can be frozen, unless otherwise stated.*

• *Cakes are cooked when they leave the sides of the tin and spring back when touched lightly with the fingertip.*

• *Cookies are usually soft even if they are cooked. They will harden on cooling.*

STEP-BY-STEP TECHNIQUES

APPLE *and* PEAR STRUDEL

FLAKY PASTRY

1¾ cups (230 g) plain flour

¼ teaspoon salt

180 g butter (salt reduced or cultured butter can be used)

¼ cup (60 ml) cold water

½ teaspoon fresh lemon juice

FILLING

3 apples, peeled, cored and quartered

3 pears, peeled, cored and quartered

1 tablespoon sour cream

freshly ground black pepper

1 sprig dill, finely chopped

beaten egg, for sealing pastry

1 TO PREPARE PASTRY: Sift flour and salt into a mixing bowl. Divide butter into four. Rub one-quarter of the butter into the flour. Add water and lemon juice and mix to a soft dough.

2 Roll out the pastry on a floured board into an oblong, about three times as long as wide.

3 Cut another quarter of the butter into pieces and place over the top two-thirds of the pastry. Fold the bottom third up and the top third down. Then roll the pastry so that the edges become sealed and the pastry has elongated. Add another quarter of butter and refold. Repeat procedure until all butter is used. Wrap dough in greaseproof paper and refrigerate for 1 hour.

4 Preheat oven to 220°C (425°F).

5 TO PREPARE FILLING: Place apples and pears in a saucepan with a little water. Bring to the boil and simmer for 10 minutes or until soft. Drain. Combine with remaining ingredients in a bowl.

Rub butter into flour.

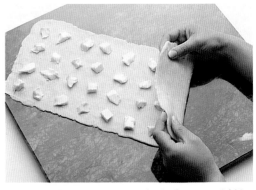

Place dobs of butter over top two-thirds of pastry and fold up bottom third.

Roll out and repeat procedure.

6 Roll out pastry on a floured board into a thin rectangle, 3 to 4 mm thick. Spread filling evenly over pastry, stopping 1 cm from all edges. Roll up tightly taking care not to break the pastry. Brush end seam with egg to seal. Place on a flat oven tray and bake for 20 to 25 minutes.

SERVES 4

Cottage Oatmeal Loaf

40 g fresh yeast

3 teaspoons sugar

2 cups (500 ml) warm milk

1½ cups (185 g) plain flour

2⅔ cups (340 g) wholemeal flour

1 teaspoon salt

2¾ cups (250 g) oats

2 teaspoons oil

1 Place yeast and sugar in a bowl with a little warm milk and stand until frothy.

2 Sift flours and salt in a large bowl. Stir in yeast mixture and remaining milk and combine to form a smooth dough.

3 Cover dough with a damp cloth or plastic wrap and set in a warm place until dough doubles in size.

4 Work in oats and oil until smooth. Turn out onto a board and knead until uniform and springy. Divide dough into two equal portions and place in greased 18 cm cake tins. Cover with a damp cloth or plastic wrap and set aside in a warm place until the dough has doubled in size.

5 Preheat oven to 200°C (380°F).

6 Cut four slits in the top of each loaf. Bake for 20 minutes, reduce to 180°C (350°F) and bake a further 15 to 20 minutes or until loaves are cooked.

SERVES 6 TO 8

Chocolate Pecan Slice

125 g butter (salt reduced or cultured butter can be used), melted

2 cups (220 g) crushed sweet biscuits

400 g canned sweetened condensed milk

¾ cup dark chocolate bits

1 cup (150 g) pecan nuts, roughly chopped

extra dark chocolate and pecans, to decorate

1 Preheat oven to 180°C (350°F).

2 Combine melted butter with biscuit crumbs. Press into the base of a 22 cm x 30 cm baking dish.

3 Pour over condensed milk. Sprinkle with chocolate bits and pecans. Bake for 30 to 40 minutes. Cool. Decorate with extra melted chocolate and whole pecans. Cut into squares.

MAKES ABOUT 48 SQUARES

Choc-Orange Ring Cake

125 g butter

¾ cup (185 g) caster sugar

2 eggs

⅓ cup (125 g) orange marmalade

¾ cup (180 ml) sour cream

1½ cups (185 g) self raising flour, sifted

¼ cup (30 g) cocoa, sifted

ICING

2 cups (300 g) icing sugar, sifted

½ cup (125 ml) sour cream

2 tablespoons marmalade

DECORATION

100 g dark chocolate, melted

1 mandarin

1 Preheat oven to 180°C (350°F).

2 TO PREPARE CAKE: Cream butter and sugar together until light and fluffy. Add eggs one at a time and beat in well.

3 Mix in marmalade. Add one-third of the sour cream and one-third of the dry ingredients alternately until all combined.

4 Pour mixture into a buttered and lined 25 cm x 7 cm ring pan and bake for 40 to 45 minutes on a rack, or until cooked when tested. Stand for 5 minutes (directly on bench) then allow to cool on a wire rack.

5 TO PREPARE ICING: Beat together all ingredients, spread over cake, then decorate with dark chocolate and mandarin segments.

SERVES 8 TO 10

COOKING WITH YEAST

• *Dried yeast can be substituted for fresh – one 7 g sachet equals 15 g fresh yeast.*

• *Liquids used in yeast cookery should not be too hot as they will kill the yeast. Also, allow the dough to prove (rise) in a warm, not hot, place for this too can kill the yeast.*

• *Crumble fresh yeast into warm milk with a little sugar and allow to 'sponge'. If bubbles appear you know the yeast is fresh and can be used. If no bubbles appear after about 10 minutes, the yeast should be discarded and a fresh batch purchased.*

Sour Cream Biscuits

SOUR CREAM BISCUITS

❧ **CULTURED BUTTER**

This is a low salt butter which has been cultured with the same bacteria often used in yoghurt. Using cultured butter gives baked goods a light taste. Try it in your favourite recipes to see the difference. Cultured butter is available at supermarkets.

2 cups (250 g) plain flour

3 tablespoons sugar

½ teaspoon bicarbonate of soda

¼ teaspoon salt

1 egg

⅔ cup (160 ml) sour cream

**40 g butter
(salt reduced or cultured butter can be used)**

extra egg, beaten, for brushing

1 Preheat oven to 220°C (425°F).

2 Sift dry ingredients into a mixing bowl. Make a well in the middle, drop in the egg and mix. Add sour cream and butter and beat well. Roll out on a floured board and cut into biscuit shapes.

3 Place on a greased oven sheet. Brush with beaten egg and pierce with a fork in several places. Bake in oven for 10 to 15 minutes until brown.

SERVES 6 TO 8

MANGO *and* CINNAMON LOAF

**125 g butter, softened
(salt reduced or cultured butter can be used)**

1 cup (200 g) sugar

1 egg

½ cup (100 g) natural yoghurt or buttermilk

1 cup (125 g) wholemeal self-raising flour

1 cup (125 g) self-raising flour

½ cup (90 g) sultanas

½ teaspoon cinnamon

2 small mangoes, puréed

1 Preheat oven to 180°C (350°F).

2 Combine butter and sugar in a bowl until creamy. Beat in egg, then yoghurt. Blend flours together and sift into mixture. Add sultanas, cinnamon and mango purée.

3 Pour into a greased loaf tin and cook in oven for 1 to 1½ hours or until golden brown.

SERVES 6 TO 8

Sage *and* Cheese Damper

TOPPING
3 tablespoons olive oil

2 onions, chopped

1½ tablespoons chopped fresh sage

30 g butter

2 cloves garlic, crushed

DAMPER
4 cups (500 g) self-raising flour

1 teaspoon salt

60 g butter

1 tablespoon chopped fresh sage or
½ teaspoon dried sage

185 g Cheddar cheese, grated

1½ cups (375 ml) soured milk and water
mixed with juice ½ lemon

1 TO PREPARE TOPPING: Heat oil in a pan and gently sauté onions until soft and tender. Stir through sage. In another pan, melt butter and sauté garlic lightly. Set aside.

2 Preheat oven to 200°C (400°F).

3 TO PREPARE DAMPER: Sift flour and salt into a large mixing bowl. Rub in butter until mixture resembles fine breadcrumbs. Stir through the chopped sage and half the cheese.

4 Make a well in the centre and stir in soured milk mixture using a knife. Gather mixture into a soft dough. Turn out onto a lightly floured surface and gather roughly into a round. Do not knead.

5 Place the round on a lightly greased baking tray and press out to about 4 to 5 cm thick. Score the surface into eighths and brush with garlic butter. Cover with onion and sage topping and sprinkle over remaining cheese. Bake for 35 minutes or until well risen and a crusty golden brown. Serve hot.

SERVES 8

Cinnamon Biscuits

125 g butter
(salt reduced or cultured butter can be used)

¾ cup (185 g) caster sugar

pinch salt

2 teaspoons powdered cinnamon

1 egg

2¼ cups (280 g) plain flour

⅓ cup (80 ml) milk

¾ cup (90 g) flaked almonds

1 tablespoon icing sugar

1 Preheat oven to 220°C (425°F). Grease a baking sheet.

2 In a warmed mixing bowl, cream butter with a wooden spoon. Add ½ cup (125 g) caster sugar, reserving the rest, and beat with butter until light and fluffy. Stir in salt and half the cinnamon.

3 Beat egg into butter mixture. Sift flour and fold in gradually to form a smooth, thick paste.

4 Dissolve rest of sugar and cinnamon in milk. Spread this over paste. Scatter with flaked almonds and dust with icing sugar. Cut into squares and set on baking sheet.

5 Bake for about 20 minutes until biscuits are slightly browned. Cool and serve.

MAKES 20

 SAGE AND CHEESE DAMPER

This damper is excellent served straight from the oven. Make it the morning of a picnic and pack it warm, wrapped in a towelling cloth, to be eaten out-of-doors. Or if you are feeling really adventurous, cook it in a bush oven. Make the dough and cut into two. Cover both rounds with the onion and cheese topping and wrap each in a double thickness of aluminium foil, leaving room for the damper to rise. Bury the foil parcels in the glowing ashes of the bush fire. Cook for 20 minutes, turning once.

STORING CHEESE

• *Buy only enough cheese for your needs, and don't use if mouldy, except blue vein cheese.*

• *Wrap cheese completely in plastic wrap or foil to prevent loss of moisture and hard patches appearing. Store in the refrigerator, with strongly flavoured cheeses stored in separate containers.*

• *Surface mould can be cut away and the cheese used as normal.*

• *Cheese is easier to grate if it has been refrigerated.*

FLAT BREAD

*The bread will keep for a
few days in the same way
as ordinary bread or can
be frozen under the same
conditions as commercial
bread.*

KNEADING

*Make sure you knead
dough well as good
kneading produces light,
well risen bread and buns.*

DATE SCONES

*Chop dates easily by
snipping them with
scissors.
Scones are cooked when
they sound hollow
when tapped.*

FLAT BREAD

40 g yeast

2 cups (500 ml) warm water

8 cups (1 kg) plain flour, sifted

130 g butter, melted

1 tablespoon sugar

2 teaspoons salt

2 tablespoons sesame seeds

1 Preheat oven to 200°C (400°F).

2 Dissolve yeast in a little of the water in a
small bowl. Cover with a cloth and set aside
for 5 to 10 minutes until mixture begins to
bubble. Place flour in a large mixing bowl
and make a well in the centre. Add yeast
mixture, remaining water, butter, sugar and
salt. Mix with a wooden spoon. Knead for
about 30 minutes until dough doubles.

3 Divide dough into 10 pieces. Roll out
each piece on a floured board until quite
thin. Place 2 circles on a baking tray with
water and sprinkle sesame seeds on top. Bake
for 20 to 25 minutes until golden brown.
Cool thoroughly and keep dry.

MAKES 10

YEAST BUNS

40g yeast

1½ cups (375 ml) milk, warmed

8 cups (1 kg) plain flour, sifted

½ teaspoon salt

5 egg yolks

1½ cups (375 g) sugar

300 g butter, melted

1 Dissolve yeast in warm milk in a large
mixing bowl. Mix in half the flour, cover
with a cloth and set aside until doubled in
size. Beat together salt, egg yolks and sugar
and add to the dough. Add remaining flour
and mix well. Knead.

2 Add butter and mix. Knead well until the
dough forms a ball. Cover and set aside.
When dough has doubled in size turn out on
a floured board.

3 Pull off about a tablespoon of dough to
shape each bun. Place dough on greased
baking tray leaving at least 6 cm spaces
between them for buns to rise. Set aside for
dough to rise, about 30 minutes.

4 Preheat oven to 220°C (425°F).
Immediately on placing dough in oven,
reduce heat to 180°C (350°F) and bake for
10 minutes. Buns will be golden and
springy to touch when done.

MAKES 15 TO 20 BUNS

DATE WHOLEMEAL SCONES

½ cup (60 g) wholemeal flour

2¼ cups (280 g) plain flour

2 teaspoons baking powder

½ cup (60 g) oatmeal

100 g butter

½ cup (90 g) brown sugar

2 eggs, beaten

1 teaspoon mixed spice

2 cups (300 g) chopped dates

⅔ cup (160 ml) milk

extra milk, for brushing

1 Preheat oven to 190°C (375°F). Grease
baking tray.

2 Sift flours and baking powder into a
bowl. Add oatmeal and rub in butter. Add
sugar, eggs, spice and dates, and combine.

3 Gradually add milk to make a smooth
dough. Knead lightly and divide into two
scones about 6½ cm in diameter and 1 cm
thick. On baking tray arrange scones close
together and brush lightly with milk. Rest
for 10 minutes. Bake for 15 minutes.

MAKES 20

Flat Bread and Yeast Buns

 **MANGO UPSIDE-DOWN CAKE**

If the cake is to be kept for a long period, pierce holes in the bottom and pour over ½ cup (125 ml) brandy every few weeks. This will keep it moist.

MANGO UPSIDE-DOWN CAKE

185 g butter
(salt reduced or cultured butter can be used)

½ cup (125 g) sugar

1 cup (125 g) hazelnuts, toasted

1 mango, thinly sliced

¾ cup (185 g) caster sugar

2 eggs, beaten

1 teaspoon instant coffee

½ cup (125 ml) milk

2 cups (250 g) self-raising flour, sifted

1 Preheat oven to 160°C (325°F)

2 Cream one-third of the butter with sugar. Spread over base and sides of a 20 cm tin. Arrange hazelnuts and mangoes decoratively on top.

3 Cream remaining butter and sugar in a bowl. Gradually add eggs and beat well. Dissolve coffee in milk, then fold into the mixture alternating with flour.

4 Pour batter into a greased cake tin, bake for 1¼ to 1½ hours, until golden. Invert cake onto serving plate and leave for 3 minutes in oven to allow brown sugar mixture to set. Remove cake from oven, cover with aluminium foil and/or a tea-towel and leave until cold. Remove from tin and wrap in foil and plastic wrap until required.

CAROB COOKIES

150 g butter
(salt reduced or cultured butter can be used)

¾ cup (125 g) brown sugar

1 egg

¼ cup (30 g) carob powder

2 cups (250 g) self-raising wholemeal flour

½ cup (90 g) raisins

½ cup (60 g) chopped walnuts

1 Preheat oven to 180°C (350°F). Lightly grease a baking sheet.

2 In a bowl, cream butter and sugar, beat in egg then stir in remaining ingredients until well mixed. Roll into walnut-size balls and place on baking sheet. Flatten lightly with fingertips or fork.

3 Bake for 12 to 15 minutes. Cool on baking sheet 2 to 3 minutes then lift onto cake rack to cool completely.

MAKES 45

OATY DATE SQUARES

1½ cups (220 g) chopped dates

finely grated rind and juice 1 orange

90 g butter
(salt reduced or cultured butter can be used)

¾ cup (125 g) brown sugar

¾ cup (70 g) rolled oats

½ cup (60 g) wholemeal flour

1 Preheat oven to 180°C (350°F). Lightly grease an 18 cm square tin.

2 Make up orange juice to ½ cup (125 ml) with water. Cook dates and rind in orange water over low heat until soft and pulpy.

3 Combine butter and dry ingredients. Press half of this mixture into prepared tin. Spread date mixture over, top with remaining oat mixture and press down. Bake for 35 to 40 minutes. Cool in tin then cut into squares.

MAKES 16

 CREAMING BUTTER

Butter should always be creamed until light in colour and texture, before adding sugar. This traps air and makes the product lighter.

FRUITY COCONUT BARS

½ cup (60 g) wholemeal flour

1½ teaspoons baking powder

½ teaspoon ground cinnamon

¼ teaspoon ground ginger

pinch ground nutmeg

½ cup (90 g) brown sugar

½ cup (90 g) sultanas

½ cup (60 g) chopped dried apricots

1 cup (90 g) desiccated coconut

2 eggs, beaten

75 g butter, melted
(salt reduced or cultured butter can be used)

1 tablespoon milk

1 Preheat oven to 180°C (350°F). Grease and line an 18 cm x 27 cm shallow tin.

2 In a bowl sift flour with baking powder and spices. Combine with sugar, fruit and coconut. Beat in eggs, butter and milk.

3 Spread mixture in prepared tin and bake for 30 minutes. Leave to cool in tin before cutting.

MAKES 16

Oaty Date Squares (top), Carob Cookies (bottom left) and Fruity Coconut Bars (bottom right)

MEASURING MADE EASY

HOW TO MEASURE LIQUIDS

METRIC	IMPERIAL	CUPS
30 ml	1 fluid ounce	1 tablespoon plus 2 teaspoons
60 ml	2 fluid ounces	¼ cup
90 ml	3 fluid ounces	
125 ml	4 fluid ounces	½ cup
150 ml	5 fluid ounces	
170 ml	5½ fluid ounces	
180 ml	6 fluid ounces	¾ cup
220 ml	7 fluid ounces	
250 ml	8 fluid ounces	1 cup
500 ml	16 fluid ounces	2 cups
600 ml	20 fluid ounces (1 pint)	2½ cups
1 litre	1¾ pints	

HOW TO MEASURE DRY INGREDIENTS

15 g	½ oz	
30 g	1 oz	
60 g	2 oz	
90 g	3 oz	
125 g	4 oz	(¼ lb)
155 g	5 oz	
185 g	6 oz	
220 g	7 oz	
250 g	8 oz	(½ lb)
280 g	9 oz	
315 g	10 oz	
345 g	11 oz	
375 g	12 oz	(¾ lb)
410 g	13 oz	
440 g	14 oz	
470 g	15 oz	
500 g	16 oz	(1 lb)
750 g	24 oz	(1½ lb)
1 kg	32 oz	(2 lb)

QUICK CONVERSIONS

5 mm	¼ inch	
1 cm	½ inch	
2 cm	¾ inch	
2.5 cm	1 inch	
5 cm	2 inches	
6 cm	2½ inches	
8 cm	3 inches	
10 cm	4 inches	
12 cm	5 inches	
15 cm	6 inches	
18 cm	7 inches	
20 cm	8 inches	
23 cm	9 inches	
25 cm	10 inches	
28 cm	11 inches	
30 cm	12 inches	(1 foot)
46 cm	18 inches	
50 cm	20 inches	
61 cm	24 inches	(2 feet)
77 cm	30 inches	

NOTE: We developed the recipes in this book in Australia where the tablespoon measure is 20 ml. In many other countries the tablespoon is 15 ml. For most recipes this difference will not be noticeable.

However, for recipes using baking powder, gelatine, bicarbonate of soda, small amounts of flour and cornflour, we suggest you add an extra teaspoon for each tablespoon specified.

USING CUPS AND SPOONS

All cup and spoon measurements are level

METRIC CUP			METRIC SPOONS	
¼ cup	60 ml	2 fluid ounces	¼ teaspoon	1.25 ml
⅓ cup	80 ml	2½ fluid ounces	½ teaspoon	2.5 ml
½ cup	125 ml	4 fluid ounces	1 teaspoon	5 ml
1 cup	250 ml	8 fluid ounces	1 tablespoon	20 ml

OVEN TEMPERATURES

TEMPERATURES	CELSIUS (°C)	FAHRENHEIT (°F)	GAS MARK
Very slow	120	250	½
Slow	150	300	2
Moderately slow	160-180	325-350	3-4
Moderate	190-200	375-400	5-6
Moderately hot	220-230	425-450	7
Hot	250-260	475-500	8-9

INDEX

Apple
    berry and buttermilk
        pancakes 20
    delicious 18
    and pear strudel 86
    and sago baked pudding 20
    yoghurt ice 74
Apricot yoghurt rice cream 17
Aubergine *see* Eggplant
Avocado soup 24

Banana
    frozen yoghurt 81
    ice cream 78
    whisk 18
    yoghurt munch 14
Barbecued beef with horseradish
    cream sauce 65
Barbecued pork kebabs 60
Béarnaise sauce 36
Béchamel sauce 50
Beef
    see also Steak
    barbecued, with horseradish
        cream sauce 65
Biscuits, savoury
    caraway cheese 84
Biscuits, sweet
    see also Slice
    carob 92
    cinnamon 89
    sour cream 88
    twists 76
Blue cheese
    dressing 25
    mousse 42
    and pecan fillet 60
Bread
    cottage oatmeal 87
    flat 90
    sage and cheese damper 89
    yeast buns 90
Brie chicken 62
Broccoli in buttermilk sauce 29
Buns, yeast 90
Butter, to clarify 64
Buttermilk
    apple and berry pancakes 20
    dressing 24
    sauce 29
Butterscotch sauce 81

Cake
    see also Slice
    caraway sour milk 85
    choc-orange 87
    chocolate torte 70
    mango and cinnamon loaf 88
    mango upside-down 92

Camembert
    chicken 62
    omelette 39
Cannelloni with spinach and
    ricotta 52
Caraway
    cheese biscuits 84
    sour milk cake 85
Carob cookies 92
Cashew-nut fudge 85
Cheddar
    cabbage rolls 31
    caraway biscuits 84
    cheesy rolls 31
    pancakes 33
    and pasta toss 46
    and sage damper 89
    soufflé 40
    soufflé potatoes 29
    and spinach turnovers 28
    vegetables in filo 31
Cheese
    see also Blue cheese; Cheddar;
        Cottage cheese; Cream cheese;
        Edam; Gouda; Ricotta
    Camembert chicken 62
    fetta spinach pie 42
    potato bake 27
    rice balls 46
    scallops with chilli tomato
        sauce 58
    tagliatelle pudding 53
    tomatoes Roquefort 29
Cheesecake, lemon 71
Chicken
    Camembert 62
    crumbed in butter 61
    and mango risotto 47
    and mushrooms 63
    saucy balls 63
Chilli
    sauce 33
    tomato sauce 58
Chocolate
    caraqué 70
    gelato 80
    ice cream 78
    mini pots 68
    orange ring cake 87
    pecan slice 87
    rum sauce 74
    sauce 81
    torte 70
Chowder, corn and prawn 57
Cinnamon biscuits 89
Citrus
    chiffon 21
    yoghurt delight 17
Coconut fruity bars 93
Coffee
    ice cream 78
    sauce 81

Coleslaw
    with buttermilk dressing 24
    fruity, with cottage cheese 14
Cookies *see* Biscuits, sweet
Corn and prawn chowder 57
Cottage cheese
    apple delicious 18
    and crab rollettes 58
    with fruity coleslaw 14
    pancakes 43
    patties 41
    stuffed potatoes 27
    turkey and ham salad 12
    vegetable bake 32
Cottage oatmeal loaf 87
Crab
    and cottage cheese rollettes 58
    pâté 56
Cream cheese
    and mango 14
    and spinach tarts 40
Crème caramel 69
Crème fraîche 56
Crêpes
    Ninette 15
    Suzette 75
Crumbed chicken in butter 61
Curry
    lamb and nut korma 60
    scallops 56
Custard sauce 20

Damper sage and cheese 89
Date
    squares 92
    wholemeal scones 90
Dip, eggplant 26
Dressing 24
    blue cheese 25
    buttermilk 24
    sour cream 49

Edam
    soyaroni 51
    and spinach salad 25
    vegetable crumble 30
Eggplant
    dip 26
    and walnut puff 30
Eggs
    see also Omelette; Quiche;
        Soufflé
    Florentine 39
    Mexican 36
    quiche Lorraine 37
    stuffed 39
    tomato and spinach
        roulade 38

Fetta spinach pie 42
Fettuccine
    with herb sauce 48
    seafood 50

Flan *see* Tart
Flat bread 90
Frozen fruit mousse 17
Frozen yoghurt, banana 81
Fruit
    brûlé 73
    coconut bars 93
    coleslaw with cottage cheese 14
    crush 17
    frozen mousse 17
    with mint and yoghurt 18
Fruit salad, tropical, with mango
    cream 14
Fudge
    cashew-nut 85
    sauce 81

Garlic cream sauce 53
Gelato
    chocolate 80
    lemon yoghurt 78
    strawberry 80
Ghee 64
Ginger
    soufflé 68
    yoghurt pears 18
Gnocchi, pumpkin with
    ricotta 52
Golden oat slice 85
Gouda
    garden salad 24
    vegetable crumble 30
Gruyère
    creamy potato bake 27
    Hollandaise, watercress 36

Honey ice cream 79
Horseradish cream sauce 65
Hot rice salad with sour cream
    dressing 49

Ice
    apple yoghurt 74
    yoghurt honey 71
Ice cream
    see also Gelato
    banana 78
    chocolate 78
    coffee 78
    honey 79
    making ice cream 77
    strawberry whip 20
    vanilla 77
Iced strawberry soufflé 16

Kebabs
    barbecued pork 60
    vegetable, with ricotta
        sauce 27
Korma, lamb and nut 60

Lamb and nut korma 60
Lasagne, pumpkin 51
Lemon
    cheesecake 71
    yoghurt gelati 78
Loaf, mango and cinnamon 88

Mango
    and cinnamon loaf 88
    cream 14
    and cream cheese 14
    upside-down cake 92
    yoghurt salad 12
Meringues in custard 68
Mexican eggs 36
Mousse
    blue cheese 42
    frozen fruit 17
Mozzarella tagliatelli pudding 53
Mussel soup with crème fraîche 56

Nut
    ricotta terrine 32
    yoghurt salad 26
    cottage loaf 87
    date squares 92
    slice 85

Omelette
    aux fines herbes 37
    Camembert 39
Orange butter 75

Pancakes
    see also Crêpes
    apple, berry and buttermilk 20
    cottage cheese 43
    savoury 33
Parmesan rice balls 46
Pasta
    basic recipe 51
    and cheese toss 46
    ricotta and veal pie 46
    with ricotta sauce 51
    with tomato and cream sauce 48
Pasta sauce
    herb 48
    ricotta 51
    tomato and cream 48
Pâté, crab 56
Pear and apple strudel 86
Pecan and blue cheese fillet 60
    see also Tart
    fetta spinach 42
    rainbow rice 42
    ricotta and veal pasta 46

Pork, barbecued kebabs 60
Potato
    bake 27
    cheesy soufflé 29
    cheesy stuffed 27
Prawns
    and corn chowder 57
    and pawpaw salad with citrus mayonnaise 13
    and scallops with tartare sauce 59
Profiteroles and chocolate rum sauce 74
Pumpkin
    gnocchi with ricotta 52
    lasagne 51
    quiche soufflé 41

Quiche
    Lorraine 37
    pumpkin soufflé 41

Rainbow rice pie 42
Rice
    apricot yoghurt cream 17
    cheesy balls 46
    chicken and mango risotto 47
    hot salad, with sour cream dressing 49
    nutty, with sweet and sour 48
    pie 42
    tropical salad 53
Ricotta
    and cannelloni with spinach 52
    nut terrine 32
    pasta sauce 51
    with pumpkin gnocchi 52
    sauce 27
Risotto, chicken and mango 47
Roquefort tomatoes 29

Sage and cheese damper 89
Salad
    see also Coleslaw
    with blue cheese dressing 25
    Edam and spinach 25
    Gouda garden 24
    hot rice with sour cream dressing 49
    nutty yoghurt 26
    prawn and pawpaw, with citrus mayonnaise 13
    tangy mango yoghurt 12
    tropical rice 53
    turkey, ham and cottage cheese 12
Salmon with sorrel cream 57

Sauce, savoury
    see also Dressing; Pasta sauce
    béarnaise 36
    béchamel 50
    buttermilk 29
    chilli 33
    chilli tomato 58
    garlic cream 53
    horseradish cream 65
    ricotta 27
    sweet and sour 48
    tartare 59
    watercress hollandaise 36
Sauce, sweet
    butterscotch 81
    chocolate 81
    chocolate rum 74
    cold coffee 81
    custard 20
    orange butter 75
    warm fudge 81
Saucy chicken balls 63
Scallops
    cheese, with chilli tomato sauce 58
    curried 56
    and prawns with tartare sauce 59
Scones, date wholemeal 90
Seafood fettuccine 50
Slice
    chocolate pecan 87
    fruity coconut bars 93
    golden oat 85
    oat date squares 92
Soufflé, dessert
    ginger 68
    strawberry, iced 16
Soufflé, Savoury
    Cheddar cheese 40
Soup
    corn and prawn chowder 57
    cream of avocado 24
    mussel, with crème fraîche 56
Sour cream
    biscuits 88
    dressing 49
Sour milk caraway cake 85
Soyaroni cheese 51
Spinach
    and cheese turnovers 28
    cottage cheese bake 32
    and cream cheese tarts 40
    and Edam salad 25
    fetta pie 42
    and rice with cannelloni 52
    and tomato roulade 38
Spun sugar 69
Spun toffee 73

Steak
    fillet with pecan and blue cheese 60
    with green pepper sauce 64
Strawberry
    gelato 80
    ice cream whip 20
    soufflé, iced 16
Strudel, apple and pear 86
Sugar, spun 69
Sweet and sour with nutty rice 48
Sweet twists 76

Tagliatelle cheese pudding 53
Tart
    see also Quiche
    cream cheese and spinach 40
    tropical yoghurt 72
Tartare sauce 59
Terrine, ricotta nut 32
Toffee, spun 73
Tomatoes
    Roquefort 29
    and spinach roulade 38
Torte, chocolate 70
Tropical fruit salad with mango cream 14
Tropical rice salad 53
Tropical yoghurt flan 72
Turkey
    creamy 63
    ham and cottage cheese salad 12

Vanilla ice cream 77
Veal
    with apple and calvados 64
    and ricotta pasta pie 46
Vegetables
    crumble 30
    in filo 31
    kebabs with ricotta sauce 27

Watercress hollandaise 36

Yeast buns 90
Yoghurt
    apple ice 74
    apricot rice cream 17
    banana munch 14
    banana whisk 18
    citrus delight 17
    with fruit and mint 18
    frozen banana 81
    gingered pears 18
    honey ice 71
    lemon gelati 78
    mango salad 12
    nutty salad 26
    tropical flan 72